378.1982
K962b

Black College Student
Survival Guide

CHICAGO, ILLINOIS

TABLE OF CONTENTS

INTRODUCTION

In 1974, I began a career as a public speaker, and through the years I have been blessed with the opportunity to speak to preschool, elementary and high school students. I have also been fortunate to speak to teachers, parents, community groups, national organizations, and churches. I enjoy speaking to all the groups, especially college students. I have had the privilege over the past two decades to speak to more than 60 colleges a year.

While I appreciate the fact that we now have Black History Month, which was initially founded by Carter G. Woodson in 1926 and named Black History Week, it's obvious that seven days was inadequate to cover more than four million years of history. Hopefully we now realize that 28 days, the shortest month of the year, is also insufficient. There have been some Black History Months where I have been in 37 states in 28 days. I wished that we could have at least chosen a month with 31 days or a month that is a little warmer than February or both. It is very difficult trying to reach so many colleges, particularly those that are not in large urban areas in the middle of a winter snow storm.

This book is the culmination of many of the speeches that I have given to college students where a myriad of issues were discussed. I believe the college years are a critical time for African American youth. It is during this period that you will literally determine your future and the type of career you will pursue. Your college years, major, GPA, and personality will determine your lifetime earnings.

During the college years many students struggle with their spirituality. Christian students love when I visit their campuses because I'm one of the few African American speakers that is unashamedly Black and unapologetically Christian! I have met an awful lot of "closet" Christians who did not want their peers, especially the rappers, muslims, nationalists, atheists, and agnostics to know they were Christians.

During their collegiate years many students find their soul mate. Unfortunately, some students either have negative encounters with the opposite sex or don't date at all. This is a very tenuous period and I take it very seriously.

While it has now been more than two decades since I was an undergraduate student, I have tried to stay current by listening to my own college educated sons, other college students, and by holding on to my own experiences at Morgan State University (MSU) in Baltimore, Maryland and Illinois State University (ISU) in Normal, Illinois.

I had the privilege of attending both a Black and White university. I can still remember what it was like as a freshman. During the first week of school the housing staff had several of us live in a lounge because they had overbooked the dormitory. After they reviewed their computer printout, they properly placed us in our rooms. It was as a college student that I began to engage my instructors and value education. Unfortunately, for so many students, college has become an extension of high school where the joy of learning is not present. For them college is just another place to secure a grade which will allow them to secure a degree which the students hope will afford them a good job.

While I cannot say that all of my professors challenged me and that I valued every course, there were enough courses and professors that triggered an insatiable desire for education and value research. I'm sure that is the reason why I didn't stop until I earned a Ph.D. I read more than 200 books a year and have written one every year. The more I learn, the more I realize I don't know, and therefore the more I study.

I'm reminded of the first university in Africa, "The Grand Lodge of Wa'at." Students entered at the age of seven and did not complete their studies until they were 47 years old. It amazes me how Americans feel they are educated with their bachelor's at 21, master's at 23, and doctorate degree by the age of 30. I have met some of these trained – not educated – people who only read when it is required.

In one of my earlier books, *To Be Popular or Smart: The Black Peer Group,* I discussed encountering peer pressure even at the college level. My friends thought that it was acceptable and Black for me to be on the track team at ISU, but not to be on the debate team. I was one of a handful of African American debaters in 1970. I am very thankful I did not succumb to peer pressure. In retrospect, my career as a public speaker began while on the debate team.

It was in college that I studied under excellent professors who engaged me in dialogue, and attended lectures where speakers challenged me about why I was there, what was my commitment to the race, and what would I give back to the larger Black community when I graduated? These were questions that I was facing for the first time and they had a major impact on my life.

In retrospect, I guess another factor that led me to becoming a speaker and writer is because I wanted to pass to the next generation the favor of all those speakers and writers who challenged me. It was not only to be the best that I could be, but also to make a major contribution to the liberation of African people.

In my travels around the country I have met some of the best and brightest African American students in the country. However, when I return to my hotel room and turn on the television, it amazes me that the drug dealer and murderer find center stage but seldom, if ever, does the media show these brilliant African American college students.

At many of the schools where I have spoken, because of the dearth of African American faculty and sometimes their lack of commitment to be involved in the lives of African American students, the students generate the phone call, the contract, confirm the date, secure the facility, promote the event, provide ground transportation, beg and plead African American students to attend, and take me out to dinner. I have truly seen some of the best and most committed African American student leaders in the country. I only wish more African American faculty would become involved.

This book was written within the political climate of the Second Reconstruction. What African Americans experienced in the 1890s is now being experienced again as we enter the 21st century. While our high school graduation numbers are increasing, the percentage of African American students entering college is decreasing. Unscientific and poor "scholarly" books like *The Bell Curve* by Charles Murray and the late Richard Herrnstein are simply warmed over renditions of William Shokley and Arthur Jensen's theories on eugenics, genetics, and race. *Someone needs to explain to racists that if African people were inferior, there would be no need to discriminate.* In almost every career where African people have been given the opportunity to participate, they have ultimately become the best.

Books like *The Bell Curve* were produced so that policy makers could make decisions about whether it was even cost effective to assist us in going to college. The assumption is that it is a waste of money to send a genetically inferior population to college. Their alternatives are orphanages, boot camps, and prisons. It is within this political environment that we see the president of Rutgers University, Frances Lawrence, Professor Lino Graglia at the University of Texas among others who agree with Charles Murray's theory that we are intellectually inferior.

In 1997, the bellwether state of California legislated Proposition 209 which abolished affirmative action. In 1996, the University of California admitted 26 African Americans to their law school. In 1997, they only admitted one and he was from the 1996 class. This was spearheaded by Ward Connerly who is on the Board of Regents who denies he is African and prefers being called Black. This was similar to the Bakke case that has had a major impact on African Americans being admitted into medical school also in California.

Texas has chosen to be the next bellwether state. The Hopwood decision has had the same deleterious effect on African American law students. In 1996, the University of Texas enrolled 31 African American law students. In 1997, there were only three. Unlike the University of California, the University of Texas saw the negative impact a culturally biased test could have on diversity and fairness. Therefore, they will admit any student in the top ten percent of their class regardless of SAT scores. Ironically, athletes and offspring of alumni still enjoy preferential treatment.

Jesse Jackson Sr. clearly states this is not a battle about overt racists, but a civil war between federal and state rights. California, Texas and there will be others are challenging the federal government. The oval office can't talk about race relations while they allow states to usurp the Constitution. Unfortunately, the states have the support of the Supreme Court led by Clarence Thomas who was admitted to Yale by affirmative action.

In the following chapters, we will look at why you want to attend college, and factors involved in selecting a college. We will then look at the habits and discipline that are necessary to become successful. Chapter four will look at retention which is only 32 percent in the African American community. Chapter five will look at Greek life for African Americans. This chapter will be followed by male/female relationships. The last two chapters will look at "DuBois' Talented Tenth" and life after college.

These are just some of the many issues I attempt to address in my speeches to college students. I have been asked so many times by the students if I had one book that encompassed all of these ideas. This book is the fulfillment of my promise to honor their requests by putting these issues into print.

I want to thank the students for the challenge. My prayer is that the following pages will address, probe, inform, and challenge you to be the best college students in America.

CHAPTER ONE

Why are you here?

It's a rewarding experience to be able to speak to a high school class during the day and then speak at a college in the evening. I love talking to students after the presentation to assess their level of Black consciousness and ascertain their future goals. My favorite question is, "What are you going to be doing when you're 30 years of age?"

Unfortunately, I have met many college students who don't have a clue as to why they are in college. Many of them have been honest and have told me that they had no alternative. I wonder how many of our 1.4 million college students are in school for that very same reason?

In volume four of my bestseller *Countering the Conspiracy to Destroy Black Boys,* there is a chapter that explores the psyche of a Black male who has graduated from high school and who is taken out in a limousine to the best restaurant in the city with his family. It is the best night of his entire life. Ironically, the next day, he experiences his greatest nightmare. He wakes up thinking about the dinner and limousine, and then looks at his high school diploma. The reality sinks in that he does not have a clue regarding what he will do in September.

For many of our students the options are simple: McDonald's, cashier at a department store, part-time at UPS, NBA, drugs, military, or college.

I wonder how many students chose college because they did not want to work at McDonald's? I wonder how many potential college students chose McDonald's because they did not want to go to college? I wonder how many African American males chose slinging boxes for UPS for four hours a day rather than attending college?

The military is aggressively seeking our men and women. I often counter their famous slogan "Be all you can be" by saying, "*You can be dead if you want to.*" They write my sons on a regular basis trying to entice them with paid college education, the acquisition of a technical skill, income, and the opportunity for international travel all expenses paid. It can sound very lucrative to an inner city kid with less than a 2.0 GPA, less than 800 on the SAT and less than 16 on the ACT, who wasn't enthusiastic about attending college anyway.

Many students have shared with me their lack of enthusiasm about pursuing college. They feel it is boring and irrelevant. I understand and empathize with their argument. I have observed too many times where enthusiastic and inquisitive kindergarten children lost their appetite for learning. Those same children in the upper grades and high school are now sitting further back in the classroom, asking fewer questions, growing more and more cynical about school.

They have concluded that school is not about learning, but about securing a grade. Very few of our youth are attending college because they don't want four additional years of what they experienced in grades K-12.

It frustrates me that we lose so many of our college students to rap, drugs, and the NBA. We live in a society that is so materialistic, that getting paid becomes the driving force. Many of our youth have concluded you will earn more money as a drug dealer than a doctor, more as a criminal than a computer programmer, more as a thief than a teacher, more as a pimp than a police officer, and more as a whore than a writer.

I often ask college students why they chose their major. For the majority income was the primary factor. Many students tell me that they are majoring in business, computer science or criminal justice and fewer in education or social work. I often ask students if they enjoy their major. Do they enjoy learning? Have they found study partners with similar majors who can engage them in dialogue? I ask them what are their aspirations in their prospective careers?

I ask the students majoring in business have they developed business plans. Have they thought about starting a business? Have they reviewed some of the case studies of some of the more successful businesses? Have they studied how Bill Gates developed Microsoft or how Reginald Lewis acquired Beatrice Foods? Some of the students look at me like I'm speaking a foreign language and honestly admit, "It's just a major. It's not my life. I'm just in it for the money."

I ask the same probing questions for those majoring in computer science. How often are you in cyberspace? Have you begun to learn how to design Web pages? Would you be interested in designing your own software? What are your plans to help the Black community become more computer literate? Once again the answers I hope for are not forthcoming. They look at me with blank stares.

I feel more confident when I talk to students majoring in criminal justice because my initial assumption is that they want to help rehabilitate the almost two million African American men and almost 300,000 African American women in prison. I become excited because I know that 90 percent of our inmates who are incarcerated are illiterate, lack a high school diploma, and possess very little knowledge about their history and culture. My assumption is that an African American majoring in criminal justice is going to restore the word *rehabilitation* and provide remedies to these problems.

Wrong again. Many of these students are not aware of those issues, but are keenly aware that the criminal justice industry is one of the largest in the nation and that cities are fighting each other about who will build the next prison. The private sector has now entered into the market place and with their addition it confirms that the objective is not rehabilitation. It's more profitable to keep people incarcerated for long periods of time. The recidivism rate is a horrendous 85 percent.

Why are you here?

I sincerely raise the question, "Why are you in college?" I naively thought that at the collegiate level the quality of the conversation especially about classes in someone's major would be different from the conversation that I hear from lay people on the streets. Some students sit in a class and listen to an hour lecture in their major that they plan on working in for the next 40 years and the first comments upon leaving the classroom is, "Who's sleeping with who? When are we going to play some basketball? What time does the party start?"

What is even more frustrating to me is when African American students talk to students from other races who are interested in more substantive discussions like articles they have read in the *Wall Street Journal, Business Week, Computer Age* or from the Sentencing Committee. They are ostracized from the larger Black community and accused of acting White.

I majored in economics. The subject fascinated me because one factor affects so many other areas. When you are required to take 15 courses in one area, it is nice to share your knowledge with someone. I remember having an 11a.m. economic class and a noon lunch before another 1p.m. class. It would have been nice if I could have sat at the lunch table with John Johnson at *Ebony magazine* and Earl Graves from *Black Enterprise* to have an intense conversation about business theories. Unfortunately that seldom happens in the African American collegiate experience.

I'm pleading with African American college students to get serious and realize that it's time to quit playing. As Arsenio Hall used to say, "Let's get busy!" As the Bible says, "When I was a child I spoke as a child, I acted like a child, but when I became a man I put away foolish things."

I have noticed when speaking to a high school class during the day and a college class in the evening that the difference was not high school and college. The difference was 12th and 13th grade. During the day I saw a 12th grader and during the evening I saw a 13th grader. *There is a difference between being a college student and being in the 13th grade.* My definition of a person in the 13th grade is someone who is unclear about their purpose or someone who is there for the wrong reasons. When students are in college because they don't want to work at McDonald's, UPS, or in the military, they are in the 13th grade. When students want to be grown without being economically self-sufficient, more concerned about reefer than reading, sex more than science, they are in the 13th grade.

My definition of a college student is one who has an insatiable desire for learning and has decided that there are certain areas that he or she would like to pursue further. College students like to explore and expand their minds to reach their fullest potential. They look at the college experience as a spring board into a career that will allow them to have an impact on our society.

Why are you here?

I really don't see much difference between the 13th grader, who has chosen a major for the sole purpose of getting paid, and a drug dealer. At one level they share the same value that money is supreme. That may explain why so many prominent African American leaders who have college degrees are now in jail for financial wrong-doings.

Many of our college students have shared with me that one of the major reasons why they went off to college is that they wanted to get away from their parents. Their definition of being *grown* was when no one tells them what to do. Ironically, being grown was not being economically self-sufficient. It was okay for their parents to continue to pay the bills; just don't tell them what to do.

They needed their own living space and wanted to live separately from their parents. The college experience provided them with no curfew and all the liquor, reefer, and other drugs they could possibly imagine . . . and as much sex as they can handle.

There are some colleges with restricted dormitory visitation. Sometimes these decisions have been made by the students. Many females have decided that they do not want males walking through their dormitories at all times of the day and have restricted it to weekends and limited hours. While there are other universities where there is co-ed living, divided by floors, therefore visitation never ceases.

There are several groups of students in this chapter that I want to look at in particular. The first being athletes. There is a percentage of African American males, and now females, who are in college because it is the natural precursor to playing in the NBA, NFL, WNBA, and ABL. I respect Major League Baseball because it has chosen to pay for the development of its athletes through the minor league system. If Dwight Gooden is a brilliant, 18-year-old pitcher in Florida who would like to pursue baseball full-time, why should he be part of a facade and attend college when that's not what he wants to do? If Dwight Gooden is clear that he would like to be a major league pitcher then there should be a system that allows him to do that. Major League Baseball provides this opportunity by allowing its athletes to enter into the minor league system.

The NBA and the NFL are more opportunistic and use colleges to develop their athletes without any compensation. I have reviewed the schedules of many of the students who are on athletic scholarship and I am reminded of slavery. It is challenging enough for a regular student to take 15 hours of classes per week and graduate on time with a respectable GPA. Some coaches require working out two hours in the morning, three hours in the afternoon, reviewing game films in the evening, traveling to the game, and playing.

Why are you here?

I won't even begin to talk about the fatigue factor of spending 4 to 10 hours daily playing in a sport that cannot pay any additional money except tuition, room, and board. The exceptional athletes have found a loop hole in the system. They have left college early to pursue their goal of playing professional sports. A few NBA athletes have eliminated college completely. When I raise the question, "Why are you here?" and you honestly tell me it's because I had no other option for going to the NBA or NFL than through this university, at least we're being honest with each other.

Please do not assume that I am not an advocate of education for these athletes. I am very much aware of the career life span of most athletes. In football it's three years, basketball four years, and baseball is five years. Only the exceptional athletes play 10 to 15 years. I am very cognizant of the possibility of a career ending in injury and of the need for alternative plans. I am fully aware of how important it is to have good communication skills, because many athletes actually earn more money in endorsements than they do on the playing field. I am more than aware of the large number of athletes who have earned millions of dollars, but because they lack business acumen, virtually retired bankrupt.

Many of the athletes that left college early or did not attend college at all have continued to pursue their education, but they have done it under their own terms. They have done it without the pressures of the collegiate experience and the slavery-type conditions. I am tremendously impressed with Juwan Howard who left the University of Michigan in his junior year because it made good economic sense, but still graduated with his class.

This was a tremendous feat because the University of Michigan is not an easy school. Just ask the students that are currently enrolled. Many of the students that were in Juwan's class who did not have the additional responsibility of playing 82 NBA games, 41 of them out of town still did not graduate with their class. Yet Juwan was able to do that by disciplining himself to study in airports, hotel rooms, airplanes, and I wouldn't be surprised if he was even studying when he was on the bench for the few minutes that he wasn't playing. If anything, I would use Juwan's example to challenge me if I were a current college student. I would tell myself if he can graduate from college under those conditions, surely I can graduate!

Each sport brings its own peculiarities. The NFL has very few of its players who have left early from the college plantation. It's a little easier for a long and lanky star like Kevin Garnett or Kobie Bryant to attempt to go pro in the NBA while it would be far more challenging for a 18 to 19-year-old still developing young man to go up against a 26-year-old man who weighs 300 pounds and can run the 40 in 4.5 seconds.

Why are you here?

Because of the physical requirements in the NFL, most players remain in college to strengthen their bodies. Students involved in sports with less money making potential i.e., swimming, wrestling, tennis, track and volleyball have a higher graduation rate.

Many of our athletes who play basketball or football dream of being one of the few selected to play pro sports. I can share horror stories with you on the "pro wannabes." These are athletes who were superior in college, but for a myriad of reasons did not make it in the pros, and are now washing dishes and hanging on corners talking about how they almost made it.

The next group of students that I want to examine are those whose parents are the driving force for them attending college. I get a little anxious when I see two and three generations of ministers, doctors, teachers, and entrepreneurs. I'm very much aware that this could have happened naturally for two generations, but my doubt increases when it moves into the third generation. I am reminded of Kahlil Gibran's poem in *The Prophet*, "Your children are not your children. They come through you but not from you and though they are with you they belong not to you." There are many parents who try to live their lives through their children. There are some parents who literally gangster their children into college and say as long as I'm paying for you to go to school I will choose the major and the college. How unfortunate that some of us majored in an area that we did not like or choose and are now working in a field that continues our foreparents' legacy, but for which we have very little passion. I wonder how many African American students are attending colleges because it was their parents' desire?

I own a communications company and would love to have my two sons work in the business since they can appreciate firsthand the lifestyle that it provided our family. I also want them to be able to monitor its activities upon my demise. Only time will tell, but I encourage them to do whatever they enjoy.

Another group of students I am concerned about are social butterflies. Some African American students choose a college because they visited it one weekend while in high school and saw the fraternity and sorority step show. I cringe when I see a student pledge one semester and flunk out the following. I wonder how many African American students attended college because they wanted to be a part of Greek life? I will discuss this in more detail in the Greek chapter.

The last group of students I want to explore are students from Africa and the Caribbean. It amazes me how students who do not live in the United States and who have greater adjustments to make out perform African American students who live here. I am very much aware of the fallacy of comparing immigrants to slaves. There are African American scholars that explain this phenomenon by contrasting immigrants from the descendants of slaves. This is a faulty argument. The problem is that you don't compare a small creme de la creme elite population who have ample resources to a larger population of primarily poor, mediocre students. It's like a country sending their five best basketball players to the U.S. to compete against a college intramural team.

I believe we can learn from this discrepancy. African Americans who live in the U.S. need to ask themselves, "What is it that students from Africa and the Caribbean are doing that we are not doing?"

What I have learned from students born in Africa and the Caribbean is that they have a very clear focus and purpose for enrolling in college. The majority of them are here to acquire as much information as possible, to secure skills that they can take back to their home country and use to empower their communities.

Why are you here? Are you here because you had nothing else to do after high school? Are you here because you did not want to work at McDonald's? Are you here because you were afraid to go to the military? Are you here because you wanted to break away from your parents but not their check book? Are you here because this was the only way you could go pro? Are you here because you wanted to be a Kappa or a Delta? Are you here because you want to get paid? Or are you here because the Black community is dying? Are you in college because you want to acquire information that you can use to empower the Black community?

Elders, women, and children are afraid to walk the streets. Drugs have become the number one industry. Teenage pregnancy is becoming rampant. Please think about these probing questions as we now look at which college is the best for you.

CHAPTER TWO

Selecting a College

Choosing a college can be a difficult task. I marvel at the criteria that many families use in selecting a college. There are more than 3,500 colleges of which 2,000 are senior colleges offering a four-year degree and 1,500 are junior colleges which offer an associate's degree. There are 106 Black colleges of which 39 make up the United Negro College Fund. These are private Black colleges. The remaining 67 are Black public colleges. Twelve of them are junior colleges.

There are some universities like Ohio State and the University of Minnesota where the student population exceeds 50,000 and there are some colleges like Rose-Hulman and Coe where the student population is less than 2,000. Most students of all races fare better in smaller more intimate environments. Sometimes the decision is based on proximity or climate. You can choose a college either in your hometown or within a 100 mile radius, or you can choose a school 3,000 miles away. When I was in high school I was offered a track scholarship to the University of Wyoming. I seriously thought about attending because it would allow me greater freedom to be away from home in Chicago. I'm glad that I ultimately chose

ISU and during my junior year participated in the exchange program with Morgan State University.

Another factor could be a public versus private college. Public colleges usually are cheaper and larger. Private colleges usually are smaller and more expensive. Some families have devised a formula on how they are going to achieve the perfect level of Blackness in White America. There are families who have decided that they will send their children to White elementary schools for the academics, Black high schools for African American culture, and White colleges to prepare them for corporate America. The assumption in their logic is that African American schools do not provide the same level of intellectual stimulation as White schools.

It also assumes that Black colleges teach more Africentricity than White schools. Ironically, my friends Cornel West, Asa Hilliard, Na'im Akbar, Molefi Asante, Oba T'Shaka, Maulana Karenga, and numerous others teach at White universities. The assumption that you have to go to a White school in order to have a greater chance of securing employment in corporate America is not accurate. My experience has been that when the Fortune 500 companies are recruiting African American graduates, they feel more confident going to Florida A&M for business graduates, North Carolina A&T for engineering graduates, Xavier for science graduates, and Howard, Hampton,

Selecting a College

Morehouse, Spelman, and so many others for students who are well rounded and possess leadership potential.

Some students choose a college based on the field of study they plan to pursue. Students that are interested in veterinary medicine may know that Tuskegee University is an excellent choice while those that want to major in film may know that Columbia University is a stellar choice.

What we have discussed thus far are decisions based on external factors: junior or senior, Black or White, small or large, near or far, and inexpensive or very expensive. External factors often play much too an important role in decision making. For instance, many adults have convinced themselves that they can't make it in one city and feel that moving to another city is going to correct the problem. Many people in relationships act very similarly. I've noticed that those that are unhappily single want to be married and those that are unhappily married want to be single. I believe that the student who possesses internal fortitude (which we will discuss in subsequent chapters) will succeed anywhere. On the other hand, I think the student that has some internal shortcomings needs to be very selective about their college choice.

For the sake of clarity, the following are the advantages and disadvantages of the types of schools that we have been discussing.

L^{OCAL} J^{UNIOR} C^{OLLEGE}

I think the local junior college is advantageous for the student who has some academic deficiencies that can be corrected inexpensively. It's also an ideal choice for the student who is not quite clear of their major. A junior college will allow them to select from a wide array of classes inexpensively.

Junior colleges also provide an excellent opportunity for someone with limited financial resources. Attending a junior college is literally like discount shopping where the student pays for two of the four years at one-tenth of the cost and will only have to pay the last two years at the higher cost.

Junior colleges also no longer see themselves exclusively as feeder schools into four-year universities, but now offer associate's degrees in many technical areas which provide the opportunity for immediate job placement for their graduates. There are many graduates of four-year schools who majored in liberal arts who have had difficulty securing employment and remain either unemployed, underemployed, or working in areas foreign to their major. Meanwhile, many junior college graduates majoring in nursing, electronics, refrigeration, computers, etc., have been able to secure employment immediately.

Selecting a College

One disadvantage of a junior college is that on some campuses the environment feels like an extension of high school and you wonder whether you are in college or in the 13th grade. Many students don't value education and had nothing else to do between 9a.m. and 3p.m. Notice that I said between 9a.m. and 3p.m. because there is a major difference between daytime junior college students and evening students. The maturity level is much greater with evening students who are often older, employed, with a family, and clearer about their objectives.

Unfortunately, many students attending junior colleges never matriculate. Only 11.5 percent of African Americans receive their associate's degree and 8 percent receive a certificate.[1] One problem students encounter is improper course selection. Colleges are run like businesses, oftentimes four-year institutions will not accept all the junior college courses. Students who plan to transfer junior college credits to senior colleges need to make sure their courses will be accepted *before* enrolling. Both colleges operate as businesses with the objective of having the student pay for as many courses as possible. Too many students have made the mistake of assuming colleges were nice educational charities.

L^{ARGE} L^{OCAL} P^{UBLIC} F^{OUR}-Y^{EAR} C^{OLLEGE}

The population at local four-year public colleges ranges from 5,000 students to 30,000 students. There is very little difference between day and evening students. The admission requirements are more stringent at four-year colleges than junior colleges with the standards being much higher for ACT and SAT scores, and the overall grade point average (GPA). Many students have to attend junior colleges because they are not admitted into four-year schools. This is a broad generalization, but the average junior college student has a GPA of 2.0 or below and an ACT score of less than 16.

In contrast, the average four-year student has a GPA of 2.0 or better average and an ACT score of 18. At the four-year college, the racial makeup is very close to the U.S. average, 12 percent African American. Many junior colleges, the African American population could exceed 75 percent depending upon the location of the college.

An African American student that attended a predominately Black high school, and a junior college, would have to adjust to now being a minority in the university, and particularly, in the classroom. Later we will discuss the dynamic of an African American student sitting in a class of 300 students, with less than 30 are African American, or where there are 30 students and less than three are African American students.

Selecting a College

One of the challenges at a large four-year school whether it's local or national is that many of the introductory courses are offered in a large lecture style environment. Students have to make an adjustment from their high school experience, where the average classroom size was 30 to this large factory style approach to education. What's worse is that some classes are taught by graduate students rather than professors. Many African American students who prefer a more personal approach to education that allows for intimacy between teacher and student won't adjust well to this format.

This is further compounded when the grade is determined solely on a midterm and final exam. I will never forget my experience at ISU where several of my classes were conducted in this format. I no longer felt like a person but a student I.D. number. I took a midterm exam with 200 multiple choice questions and my letter grade was posted on a computer printout outside the classroom door. What were my weaknesses or strengths? Which answers were wrong? Some professors go over tests in subsequent lectures. If they don't, it is the student's responsibility to ascertain which questions were answered incorrectly because you may see the same questions on the cumulative final exam.

The local four-year college has a commuter, transient atmosphere. Very few of these colleges have dormitories and at best they house only 10 percent of the student population. The majority are commuter students. They drive or take public transportation to the university, stay for a succession of classes and either work or return home. Students who may not be as fortunate to have their classes in succession are often found in the library or in the cafeteria. Most commuter students are not actively involved in social aspects of campus life.

My experience as a public speaker is that the audience is drastically different when I speak at a commuter four-year college versus if I speak at a non-commuter college. If the coordinator schedules me for noon their only chance at gathering an audience is the random possibility that an adequate number of students do not have a class at noon, but are remaining on campus because they have a later class. If the coordinator chose to have the program in the evening most daytime students would not stay on campus to attend, and the evening students only come to campus for their classes. Their schedule is very structured, therefore very few evening students are found in the cafeteria, library, or available for extra-curricular activities.

One major advantage of attending a local four-year college is that its less expensive because it's state supported. Also, because it is local you forego dormitory expenses and continue to enjoy home-cooked meals and other accoutrements from familiar surroundings.

Selecting a College

The university is a microcosm of the corporate community and prepares the African American student for multiculturalism, diversity, inclusion, competitiveness, and discrimination. I have observed there is a closer relationship between theory and practice among students who attend local four-year colleges versus other colleges. Most students attending local four-year universities also work in that particular city. They have a daily opportunity to compare their university with their workplace. Students living in dormitories in a desolate college environment, often work in a university position. They have less appreciation and understanding of the corporate culture.

Many working commuting students also have other family responsibilities which extend the traditional four-year experience. Many students who are gainfully employed use college to enhance their climb up the corporate ladder. They may not feel as pressured as someone who is an exclusive college student hoping upon graduation to secure employment.

LOCAL FOUR-YEAR PRIVATE UNIVERSITY

Local four-year private universities are smaller than the public ones, and in most cases the admission requirements are more stringent. Because they are private, they are also more expensive. They are viewed as the creme de la creme and are very respected by the corporate community and the larger society. Students that graduate from these universities are highly regarded. Examples of these universities in my hometown include the University of Chicago, DePaul, Loyola, Roosevelt, and Northwestern. While tuition at a public four-year college ranges from $3,000 to $10,000, the figure is twice that amount or more for some private colleges.

The admission requirements to a school like the University of Chicago are very demanding. The median ACT score hovers near 26 and the median SAT scores is 1,300. Students that are very serious about their majors and are knowledgeable about the experts in the field gravitate to certain private schools because they have departments that are world renowned, and they have Nobel Prize winning professors who are highly respected in their field.

Unlike the public four-year college where you had a lecture hall experience of over 300 students, in most private colleges 30 students would be considered a large class and 13 average. The racial composition of these schools is less than half our general population of 14 percent due to financial and academic requirements.

I have had the privilege of speaking at many of these private colleges and have enjoyed engaging some of the brightest minds in Black America. In a subsequent chapter titled, "DuBois' Talented Tenth," we will discuss that one student is not better than the other, solely based on one scoring 16 on the ACT and the other scoring 32. When the police pull you over late at night and prepare another Rodney King style beating, I don't think they will ask you do you attend a junior college or Harvard? or "What was your ACT score?"

I have always been proud of the student who has not only satisfied the admission requirements of these schools, but who is also committed to the liberation of African people. We don't need anymore "educated fools." We need students who realize "to whom much is given, much is required."

It's even more rewarding to meet some of these students who came from low income, single parent homes. They disprove the writings of pseudo scholars who suggest that "melanin-ated" people, from low income single parent homes are not intellectually competent.

The environment at many of these private four-year colleges can be stressful and borders sometimes on the eccentric. Some White students try to convince African American students that they are different. Unfortunately, some African American students thought that different was meant to be complimentary. In reality the White students' racism was so thick and so narrow that they have a monolithic view of African Americans. When African Americans fall outside their narrow racial scope rather than widening their understanding of African Americans, they remove them from the Black race and attempt to make them "race neutral" because they cannot fathom that an African American could score greater than 26 or 1,300 on a culturally biased test.

I think that attending this type of university is an excellent opportunity for an African American student who is well grounded in his/her history and culture. Unfortunately, I have seen too many students who were ahistorical, apolitical, and acultural graduate thoroughly confused and suicidal.

S TATE F OUR-Y EAR C OLLEGE

I'm a graduate of Illinois State University which is approximately 120 miles from Chicago. When I attended ISU there were approximately 20,000 students of which 1,000 were African Americans. Today ISU student population remains about the same. Because it is state supported tuition, room and board are relatively inexpensive. The average cost for a year range between $8,000 to $15,000 in contrast to the private schools which range between $18,000 to $30,000.

Our class was the first that had 1,000 African American students. Previously the African American population ranged between 50 students and 300 students. The retention rate was much greater when the class was smaller. ISU like many public universities increased the African American population, but it appears they were more concerned about numbers than retention. Only 25 percent of our class graduated in four years. Some schools have a revolving door atmosphere. Their concern is filling their 1,000 African American students quota.

For many African American students who attend schools where they are the racial minority, they experience culture shock. For an inner city, high school graduate to sit in a class where he/she is the only African American can be traumatic. Living in a dormitory with a White roommate requires cultural adjustment. Prom coordinators at integrated high schools have to decide what type of music is going to be played at the prom. The same decision is made on a daily basis in dormitory rooms.

The decorations on the walls remind me of the United Nations. On the African American wall there is Snoop, Tupac, Dr. Dre, and Biggy Small. On the White wall there is the Rolling Stones, Guns N Roses, and Tonic. Visitation can be a sensitive issue. If African American students survive this first year, they can ask the housing department for an African American roommate the following year.

Unfortunately, many African American students don't make it to the sophomore year because they are unable to make the cultural adjustments. I have seen African American students choose studious White roommates because they feel that socially inclined African American roommates negatively affect the quality and quantity of study hours.

Many students tell me they chose a state school or an integrated school because it's a microcosm of the larger society and the corporate world. Ironically, I have seen within the large state college a miniature Black college environment. *60 Minutes* did an exposé on this phenomenon, and featured Duke University. Duke is a large, private college in North Carolina with an African American population of less than 10 percent. African American students have carved out their own little world. They have breakfast, lunch, and dinner together. Their social activities and parties are primarily sponsored by their fraternities and sororities. You would think when you visited Duke or ISU that you were visiting a miniature Howard or Hampton University.

White students who are race-centered and only see the world from their perspective were shown on *60 Minutes* indicting African American students for separating themselves from the larger population. When you point at someone at least three fingers are pointing back at you, and White students need to look at themselves around the cafeteria. While they see four tables with 100 Black students, they need to see the 900 White students seated in similar configurations.

Were Black students the only students that segregated themselves from other students? Did not White students also segregate themselves from Black students? How many White students voluntarily initiated sitting with their Black friends, if they had any? Should Black students be required to maintain their "Black membership" by only eating with African American students? Should Black students be labeled "Oreos" or "Uncle Toms" if they prefer occasionally to sit with White students? Are Black students required apart from class time to spend all of their waking hours with African American students? Should Black students be removed from the African American population if they are found in a White or Asian study group? Or seen in the library with non-African American students? If this is the case then why did they attend an integrated school? Why didn't they attend a Black college?

One of the benefits of a state school is its close proximity to your hometown. This allows more frequent visits and less expensive. Many students who've chosen more distant schools may not be able to visit during Thanksgiving or spring break. While I'm glad I did not choose the University of Wyoming 3,000 miles away, I was very concerned about students at ISU who went home every week. How could they possibly find their niche and make adjustments if they never gave it a chance? I am also concerned about students who have a significant other back home who they visit every weekend. In my opinion they miss a very important part of the college experience by never being on campus on the weekends. To me this type of student would have been better off going to the local four-year college.

In a subsequent on relationships, we will look at this dynamic further. How unfortunate for students to miss one or more years of campus life because they were in love with someone back home only to break up with that person and never be able to recoup the rich campus experience.

I want to contrast my ISU experience with that of a smaller four-year college in a more remote area of the state. I had the opportunity to speak at the University of Minnesota in Mound. It was an experience that I will never forget. While the school is public, it is much smaller than ISU. It has less than 3,000 students. The year I spoke there they had less than 20 African American students, fourteen females and six males. The school was approximately five hours from Minneapolis which made it very difficult for students to visit on a regular basis.

Because Mound was five hours from Minneapolis it was impossible for African American students to listen to a Black radio station. Oftentimes we take for granted access to a Black radio station. This was traumatic because literally there were no Black radio stations to inform you of the highlights in the African American community including what new Black music was being released. All you had were old cassettes and CDs. This problem was further compounded by a lack of access to Black hair care products, beauticians, and barbers. They had to become each other's beauticians and barbers.

I have spoken at numerous schools like this and it always amazes me when I see African American students there because it reinforces the fact that African people are everywhere. We are not a monolithic people, not all of us live in New York City. Yet our desires, aspirations and fears, are similar whether we live in Mound or Memphis, Cheyenne or Chicago, North Dakota or New York, Boise or Baltimore, or Wyoming or Washington, D.C.

Many of my friends who are committed to trying to find schools which provide financial assistance for African American students have told me that they have had greater success placing students in these remote White colleges than in historically Black colleges. They have informed me it's not their preference, but if the student does not have the financial resources, and Morehouse and Spelman are not offering financial assistance, and the student wants to attend college, these remote White schools have financial resources. Many high school counselors believe if an African American student is serious about college then they have the discipline to matriculate at the local junior college or an Ivy League school.

B LACK C OLLEGES

The discussion of Black colleges will encompass small and large, public and private, commuter and residential. It will only encompass the 94 senior colleges. The 12 junior colleges were in the previous section. Black colleges have student populations ranging from as small as 750 to as large as 13,000 at Southern and Howard University. Since integration, (Brown vs. Topeka 1954, Civil Rights Act 1964, Adams decision 1973) the percentage of African American students attending Black colleges has declined.

In 1976, 18.6 percent of African American students (175,411) attended Black colleges. Presently, 16 percent (210,876) attended Black colleges.[2] While this percentage has declined due to students having greater options, the aggregate number of African American students at Black colleges has increased. The strength of Black colleges is that only 16 percent of all African American college students attend; they produce 28 percent of all graduates. Their mission is to take African American students where they are and produce the best out of them.

Naysayers take the position that their retention rate is greater at Black colleges because the curriculum is less demanding. That argument flies in the wind when we see that 25 percent of African Americans who receive their Ph.D. at White colleges earn their undergraduate degrees at Black colleges.[3] If Howard is inferior then what prepared these students for their doctorate from Harvard? If Spelman is inferior how did they secure their graduate degree from Stanford? If Prarie View is inferior how did they secure their graduate degree from Princeton? In addition, Black colleges with a limited number of graduate schools produce more than eight percent of the doctorates.

Black colleges are not monolithic. There is a wide array of experiences at these 94 senior colleges, beyond the variance in population. There are schools like Hampton and Spelman that have endowments in the tens of millions of dollars, and there are other schools that are struggling to buy enough toilet paper and produce enough hot water for showers.

There are Black colleges with a 95 percent or greater African American population while some schools like Tennessee and Kentucky State after integration struggle to exceed 50 percent. There are some highly competitive schools like Morehouse, Spelman, Hampton, and others where less than 20 percent of the applicants are admitted. Others will admit you upon completing the application. There are Black colleges in large, metropolitan areas like Atlanta, Washington, D.C., and Baltimore while there are others in the middle of a cotton, sugar cane, or tobacco plantations.

Some people feel that going to a White college improves your employment opportunities in corporate America but when the Fortune 500 companies are recruiting African American graduates, they feel much more confident visiting African American colleges. The successes of Florida A&M, North Carolina A&T, and Xavier are stellar examples.

I had the opportunity to attend a Black college during my junior year through an exchange program between ISU and Morgan State University (MSU) in Baltimore, Maryland. That was a very significant year of my life. It was at MSU that I became Africentric and committed to the Black liberation struggle. It was there I met my best friend and became a vegetarian.

There were stark differences between attending ISU, a White school where only one-tenth of the population was African American and MSU where the reverse was true. I also witnessed some of the pitfalls of Black colleges. At

Selecting a College

ISU we wanted to increase the numbers and percentages of African American students enrolled. We felt that with greater numbers we could have a greater impact on the university. It was very difficult for us at ISU to elect an African American student body president when we only had 1,000 votes out of 20,000. MSU did not have that dilemma. The numbers were in their favor. Yet we actually had more unity at ISU than at MSU. This was disappointing

Why is it that we seem to have a greater unity when the numbers are not in our favor? In a subsequent chapter on "DuBois and the Talented Tenth" we will investigate this question. I was also very disappointed that because I was majoring in economics and business that a large percentage of my instructors were non-African American. One of the major reasons I wanted to attend a Black college is that I wanted to be mentored by more African American professors because there were so few at ISU. While the population of African American students attending Black colleges is usually more than 90 percent, the percentage of African American faculty members is oftentimes below 50 percent. And in some cases it is non-existent in the math, science, and business departments.

It is disheartening when African American students take statistics, calculus, chemistry, or physics from foreigners who oftentimes have a tremendous English language deficiency. It is hard enough for many African American students to learn statistics from their "homey" much less from someone that they can barely understand.

There is a shortage of African American teaching faculty, specifically in math and science. This nationwide shortage is exacerbated at Black colleges due to the pale comparison in salaries they can earn at White universities.

It is unfortunate that we have stronger Black Studies programs at White colleges than Black colleges. Many Black college officials tell me that they teach Black Studies in all of their courses. Some tell me that their students don't need Black Studies because they need to prepare themselves for corporate America. Lenita McClain who was on the editorial board of the Chicago Tribune and Diana Green a brilliant business woman for Duquesne Electric both committed suicide because they didn't understand White supremacy.

The classic statement that I hear from some of these Black college officials who have been in administration for the past 30 years and have no place to go but retirement, Heaven, or Hell is "This is the way we've always done it." I cringe when I hear that statement because that's why we are in the state we are in, and it's time to change.

It disappoints me that a stronger Black Studies Program exists at Ohio State University than Central State or Wilberforce University. There is a stronger Black Studies program residing at Temple University than Lincoln or Cheyney. Why don't Black colleges employ Asa Hilliard, Na'im Akbar, Cornel West, Maulana Karenga, Molefi Asante, or Oba T'Shaka to name a few? Some of my friends above have told me that it was not just the money, but it was also the administration that resisted Africentricity and the principles of the Nguzo Saba (Unity, self-determination, collective work and responsibility, cooperative economics, purpose, creativity, and faith) and Maat (Truth, justice, order, harmony, balance, righteousness, and reciprocity.)[2]

Many African American students would love to attend a Black college, but they received greater financial aid from White colleges. Eighty-eight percent of African American students require financial aid.[4] There is fierce competition not only for African American students, but athletes, and scholars.

F ACTORS T O B E C ONSIDERED

Let's review the factors that you need to consider in the selection of a college and/or as you consider transferring from one school to another:

1) What are the admission requirements?

2) What is the cost?

3) What is the retention rate of African American students?

4) What kind of financial assistance is provided?

5) What type of academic support is provided?

6) What is the percentage of African American students enrolled?

7) What is the percentage of African American faculty?

8) What type of social life do African American students have?

9) Is there access to a local Black radio station?

10) What is the status of African American fraternities and sororities?

11) Is there an African American studies department?

12) Is there an active Black Student Union?

13) What is the racial climate on campus?

14) What positions of leadership do African American students and African American faculty members possess?

15) How accessible is the university to an urban area?

16) How many African American speakers visited the

campus in the past 12 months?

17) What departments have received national acclaim?

18) What percentage of graduates were placed in positions that complemented their major?

19) What are the dormitory visitation rules?

20) How competitive is the school in sports?

21) How safe is the university?

22) Is the university fiscally sound?

Now that we have selected the best college for us, lets read about the habits and discipline necessary to graduate and become successful.

CHAPTER THREE

Habits and Discipline

When I attended ISU in 1970, 1,000 African American students enrolled as freshmen. Four years later only 254 graduated. Did we graduate because we were smarter? Was it because most of us came from two parent, middle income families? Was it because the majority of us attended suburban high schools, or magnet schools? Was it because we took advanced placement and honors classes?

Have you ever wondered why there can be two athletes on the same team with similar abilities and one makes the high school or college or professional team and the other doesn't? Have you ever looked around at your friends and noticed that while you all run together, some seem to achieve more than others? People often ask me how I have been able to write a book per year. This book is my 18th book and they may still be working on their first. It's not as if I have more time, so they don't quite know what is the difference.

This chapter is a component of a much larger subject that my friend Dennis Kimbro wrote about in his excellent book, *What Makes the Great, Great.* In my own study of what makes great people, I have noticed several factors: 1) they have excellent habits; 2) they are very disciplined; 3) they have a positive attitude; 4) they are masters of time management; 5) they are very selective of their friends; 6) they look for mentors, and 7) they believe in God.

The first year of most endeavors is the most challenging. Many people describe the first year as the "make it or break it year." Many high-school principals have told me that the greatest percentage of dropouts is not in the 11th or 12th grade, but in the 9th grade. The business failure rate is 30 percent for most businesses in the very first year. The divorce rate is very similar to the first year having the greatest number of casualties.

Unfortunately the same is true for college students. Their first year is crucial and often unsuccessful. Retention data illustrates the largest attrition rate explains in the freshman year. Charles Cherry explains in the excellent book, *Excellence Without Excuse*, that Black college freshman have the hardest time of all racial groups. "Only 14 percent of Black freshmen achieved a B average after the first semester compared to 47 percent of White freshmen."[1] Forty percent of African American students have less than a C average after their first year.[2] That means at most colleges, forty percent of African Americans are on probation if they return for their sophomore year. While African American students who survive the tumultuous first year compare favorably with their White counterparts during the latter years, their GPA seldom catches up with their White peers. I could be more succinct and say that the first sixty days are the most critical. In most classes within 60 days you have already taken a midterm exam. If you score a D or an F on the midterm and an A or B on the final, the best case scenario is that you will receive a C. Students who receive C's, D's or F's the first two years and A's and B's the latter two years will unfortunately earn an overall GPA of 2.0 or less.

As we have already discussed, some African American freshmen experience culture shock when they are introduced to college life. For the African American student who has lived in a densely populated Black community to now be enrolled in a highly integrated college in the midst of corn fields takes some adjustments. For students who are used to seasoned food the cafeteria can be unappealing. To have a roommate who does not look like you, has never seen anyone who looks like you, and has different musical taste makes it that much more difficult to acclimate oneself. Many students need more than 60 days to adjust. The fact that no one tells them what to do, when to do it, or how to do it requires a huge adjustment. It has become clear to me that those people that became successful regardless of their new environment bring their habits, discipline, positive attitude, time management skills, selection of their friends, mentors, and belief in God to every situation.

In Egypt, formerly known as Kemet (kmt), the educational cornerstone was, "Man know thyself." Many people can live their entire lives and never *know* who they are. Many people can live their entire lives and never develop good habits and become disciplined.

I have given exercises to elementary students where I wanted them to just look at me. I wanted them to keep their eyes focused on me, without laughing, smiling, or speaking. Many of them were unsuccessful after 60 seconds. Children's minds are undisciplined, impulsive, and self-centered. The mind directs our overall behavior. Thank God when the brilliant neurosurgeon Ben Carson was operating on Siamese twins he had discipline to focus his mind on his patients for 17 hours.

More than why they are on campus, some students lack identity. They have not done an inventory of their assets and liabilities, strengths and weaknesses. A basketball player knows his strength is dribbling to the right example before he/she takes the shot or drives to the hoop. Knowing that, the defense will try to force him to dribble to the weaker side. We understand that in sports and about other people, but lack comprehension for ourselves.

I would like for you to answer the following questions, What are your better subjects? Do you have a large vocabulary? Do you have good writing skills? Do you have a good math background? Are you a good test taker? Do you prefer an oral or written exam? Do you study bet ter in groups or alone? How well do you manage your time? How do you respond to defeat? Do you have a positive attitude? How do you accept criticism? Do you have a criterion for selecting your friends? Who is your mentor? Do you have a good work ethic? Do you attribute your success to ability, effort, luck, or the nature of the task?

Many of us deceive ourselves. We look good on the outside but are very shallow on the inside. My pastor, Jeremiah Wright Jr., reminds our congregation that everybody smiling is not happy and you don't know what people are experiencing on the inside. This reminds me of Michael Jackson's challenge that we need to think about the man in the mirror and the following poem.

THE MAN IN THE GLASS

You get what you want in your struggle for self
and the world makes you king for a day.
Just go to the mirror and look at yourself
and see what that man has to say
for it isn't your father or mother or wife
whose judgement upon you must pass.
The fellow whose verdict counts most in your life
is the one starring back from the glass.
Some people may think you a straight shooting chum

and call you a wonderful guy
but the man in the glass says you're only a bum
if you can't look him straight in the eye.
He's the fellow to please never mind all the rest
for he's with you clear up to the end.
And you've passed your most dangerous, difficult test if
the man in the glass is your friend.
You may fool the whole world down the pathway of years
and get pats on the back as you pass
but your final reward will be heartache and tears
if you've cheated the man in the glass.

Anonymous

In studying great people, the most important factor that I have observed is how well they use their time. Whether you are Black or White, male or female, everyone has 24 hours per day. And the way the game of life is played God has given us all talents. Matthew 25 teaches us that some receive five, others two, some one. The game of life is played with 24 hours and talents. The winner is determined based on how you use your time to develop your talents. The more talents you develop, God will reward you with more.

Habits and Discipline

For many of us, because we lack discipline we need someone to artificially create our schedule because many students waste precious hours. It has always been ironic to me how someone could take 18 hours, work part-time, or be an athlete and earn a higher GPA than someone only taking 9 to 12 hours with no extracurricular activities. People who lack discipline and good habits, have no idea how much time they waste daily.

I observed as a student in college and now as a college speaker, that many students are not aware of time wasters. For many students wasting time begins early in the morning. As a result of staying up late at night they oversleep and miss their 8a.m. class. For many, the longer they sleep the more they need. There are some students who are sleeping 10 to 12 hours daily, which is half the day. Other students are only sleeping six hours daily. It would be an interesting study to compare sleeping time of students who matriculated to those on probation or expelled.

The time allocated for early morning activities also should be explored. There are some students who literally jump out of bed and in 15 minutes have dressed, eaten breakfast, and are walking to class. It may take other students an hour or longer to get out of bed, primp, and eat breakfast.

There are some students who realize that breakfast is just that – breaking a fast. You don't break a fast with ham, eggs, potatoes, and pancakes. Your body is looking for food that is alive. Juice, fruit, and granola give the body all that it needs to have a very productive day. Many students after their big breakfast are found sleeping in class.

There are some students who combine breakfast with gossiping and have an hour conversation at the table before class. At week's end they are not cognizant of time wasted in bed, the mirror, and cafeteria.

I often wonder if some sisters are going to class or a fashion show? In the first chapter I described the difference between being one of 20 African American students at the University of Minnesota at Mound and being one of 12,000 at Southern University in Baton Rouge, La. I'm sure the sisters in Mound, Minn. spend less time primping in the mirror than their peers at Southern University. While some may quickly counter there were few to impress at Mound, I believe greater priority should be allocated to developing your brains than your hairstyle.

As we progress through a typical day for students, who have an 8a.m. class followed by an 11a.m. class with a two hours later. This is our second critical test of time management. Do they stroll back to the dormitory, chill, talk to their friends, listen to rap, and watch television? Do they go to the Student Union, hang out with friends or play pool? Some students have chosen to major in bid whist and minor in spades.

Do they hang out on campus depending upon the weather? College students have created the "corner" on campus. Or do they go to the library or meet with their professor or their mentor? I believe there is a fine line between those who graduate and those who don't, and how these two hours are utilized could be the watershed factor.

In the following chapter on retention, we'll discuss this idea further, because I'm making a gross assumption that students are attending class. For many students, their failure was a result of poor attendance. I've always wondered what is more important for a college student than attending class? Many college students have given me a myriad of answers. All of which in my opinion are unacceptable, but make very good sense to students who lack priorities.

It is now lunchtime and because the food is available many students feel obligated to eat three meals a day plus snacks. While some students complain about the food. Most students actually gain weight. I've observed students who eat in 10 minutes, but talk until the cafeteria closes. I've sat at some lunch tables and heard students say they were going to the room to take a nap. I don't know if it's because they have been sleeping so much that their body needs more sleep. Was it the food? Did they not have anything to study? Had they mastered all their subjects? Why would a young adult need a nap in the middle of the day while their grandparents are working from sunrise to sunset? But the students who have good habits and discipline have chosen to study in their dormitory room or in the library.

Just as we saw problems in the earlier part of the day where there was a gap in classes, a student could have a 1p.m. class followed by a 4p.m. class with the same two problematic hours between. There are some students who take evening classes and have the entire day free until 5p.m. when they have a three hour class that meets once a week. It takes a great degree of discipline to be productive from 9a.m. until 5p.m. and many of our students have had poor habits do not use that time very wisely. I would encourage all students at the end of each day to audit their 24 hours.

I have talked with students on probation due to poor grades who decide to make major changes for the following semester. One of their changes was to eliminate partying. I have always had concerns about that decision, not because I'm a party animal, but I have often wondered whether they were going to actually study on Friday or Saturday night from 10p.m. to 3a.m. From my perspective, I would think a student could still attend the party and make sure that before and after the party they were back in the books.

Unfortunately, because of poor time management, the five hour party has a much more lasting effect on some people than others. I liked to party, but I never had to be high to enjoy myself. For many people the party began at 7p.m. when they were getting high. Some people can't party unless they are high. Some people can't dance without drugs. Some people can't laugh without liquor.

I used to party in college until 2a.m., but the following morning I was up and ready to study again. Many students partied until 2a.m., partied at the after-set until 5a.m., had "after-sex" until 7a.m. They slept from 7a.m. til 3p.m. When they got out of bed they had a hangover, an upset stomach, sluggish, and were unable to study, but they were ready for the next party.

The organizations only had parties on Fridays and Saturdays when I was a freshman at ISU, but before I graduated the parties had extended from Wednesdays through Sundays. I guess some people understand their personalities and know that for them a party is more than a five hour experience. For them it has long range implications and because they lack discipline it's better to eliminate parties.

While there is some merit to external change without internal virtues, the desired results may not occur.

Eliminating partying is not synonymous with increasing study. I remember when our sons were younger, we had designated days when there was no television viewing. Unfortunately, studying did not increase. One of our sons chose to go to sleep earlier in hopes that morning would arrive sooner and his television privileges could be restored.

Students who lack discipline are in for a rude awakening when they leave home for the first time and go off to college. There is so much free time available. There are 168 hours in a day minus the average course load of 15 hours, which leaves 153 hours to be allocated. This may be the most important point in the book. The million dollar question is how well do you use these 53 hours? I firmly believe those students who do a better job managing their 153 hours per week not only will fair better in college, but also in life. In contrast, other students wake up late and ask "What's happening?" because they don't know. Life passed them by.

In addition to time management, students need to learn money management. I have met students who told me they had one dollar in their pocket and they've had it for the entire week. They have done well. I have talked to other students who told me they spent $100 that week and were calling their parents for more. I have met some students whose telephone bills should allow them to become stockholders for AT&T, MCI, or Sprint. I have met other students who realize the beauty of the Internet and are now sending E-mail messages home to their parents. Others have decided their rites of passage into adulthood is to sign up for every credit card that has been mailed to them and live in debt forever. How unfortunate that college students who are supposed to be literate, and yet do not read the fine print where the interest rate is 18 to 23 percent annually. How disappointing for a student who did not graduate from college, but has telephone bills which exceed $2,000 and credit card bills over $5,000. They majored in foolish debt.

Some students are not aware that pizza every night can be expensive. It's cheaper to buy a bag of microwave popcorn. Some students have become stockholders in vending machines. They will spend $1.00 on a can of soda in the vending machine that could have been purchased at a discount store for one-third the price. The same applies for candy bars and potato chips. Students would be amazed at how much they spend annually in vending machines. Just as many students cannot explain how they spend their time, they also can't explain how they spend their money. Most college students don't have budgets, but then neither do their parents.

Just as I encourage students to develop a schedule, I also encourage students to develop a monthly budget.

Students should understand the difference between a need and a want. If students do not learn this early then they will become victims of debt like many of their parents. They will work in corporate America and spend more than they earn. They will be unable to ever quit their job because they're indebted to Visa, a car note, and a mortgage.

One of the big decisions that students must make is whether they will stay on or off campus. Many students are quick to convince their parents that it's cheaper to live off campus. But if students are honest they will confess that the major reason why they're desirous of this move is because it gives them greater freedom to entertain. They will have larger quarters with no visitation restrictions. They do not like the food, their roommate, or living on a floor with strangers and sharing the bathroom.

While I appreciate the above, it has always amazed me how the same people that moved off campus because they did not like the food are begging students for their meal ticket. Many off-campus students specifically males discover McDonald's is not cheap. While the sandwich may cost $2.00 when they add everything to it including tax, they have spent over $5.00 and that's only one meal. They have two meals plus a snack to go.

In addition, McDonald's may not be the most nutritious place to eat every day of the week. While many students did not like the food on campus they seldom went grocery shopping. Few students have discipline to return home on a daily basis and make a pot of greens, beans, meatloaf, potato salad, spaghetti, salad, and fried chicken. In addition, this is very time consuming and may not be advantageous for your GPA.

Another factor to consider is the distance between your apartment and the university. On most campuses the commute is going to require an automobile. Students are quick to convince their parents that it's cheaper to buy an automobile than to pay dormitory expenses. This is a very convenient argument for students who wanted a car at the very outset and now have an excellent rationale. This car will not only be used for the commute, but also to visit other campuses around the country.

Some students are not fully cognizant that automobile expense exceeds the purchase. Cars need gas, oil changes, tune-ups, batteries, tires, brakes, and other parts. There is a safety concern when students travel hundreds of miles to visit their friends at other campuses. From a parent's perspective I have reminded my sons that you have now placed your life in the hands of the driver, so be absolutely sure the driver is drug free and alert.

Most off-campus students need roommates to share expenses. They are dependent upon these students to adhere to the financial obligations. Many students don't meet their financial responsibility because they lack budgeting skills and are irresponsible. Some students only pay rent, but forget that household expenses include utilities and food. Ironically, the students who are most delinquent seem to eat the most. Some students leave school due to probation and roommates become responsible for the full amount.

Living with a roommate in a dormitory room or off-campus is very similar to marriage. Some people can like and love each other, but simply can't live together. When three to four people come together to share a house, this can be very complicated. Some roommates want to bring their friends over to spend the night and allow them to consume food they did not purchase. It becomes a real nightmare for the student who not only bought most of the food, but would also like to study in their own house.

I have also observed many off-campus students who did not have transportation and were dependent upon their roommates. They were disproportionately absent from class and could be found waiting for a ride home in the Student Union. Satan can make off-campus living very appealing, but it could have a deleterious effect on your retention.

One of the major factors I have observed among great people beyond time and money management is the selection of their friends. I often remind high school students "the group you run with will be the group you end up with or the fruit does not fall too far from the tree." This is also a major factor in determining the success of college students.

In the following chapter on retention we will discuss how Asians and other groups use their friends and cooperative study groups to improve academic achievement. Positive peer pressure that reinforces academic achievement is lacking in the African American community. Many of our students seem to have greater loyalty to their friends than their grades.

I would like for you to look carefully at your closest friends. Do you think they are going to graduate? What is their current GPA? Why are your friends in college? Do they have a clear purpose? How well do they manage their time? How well do they manage their money? Do they have a personal relationship with God? Do they understand and practice Africentricity, Maat, and the Nguzo Saba? Do they consume liquor and other drugs? Are they sexually active and to what extent? Do they have a criminal behavior? Are they neat? Do they possess good study habits? What is their family background? How do you benefit from the relationship? Is the relationship reciprocal or toxic? Does your friend respect your opinion? Are you easily influenced by your friend? Does your friend have your back? Do you understand the difference between a friend and an associate? Do you trust your friend with your money and your possessions? What other type of people does your friend associate with? How do your other friends and relatives relate to this friend?

I know these are tough questions and most of us don't interview our friends to this magnitude. Unfortunately we don't study our future spouses at this magnitude either and that's why our divorce rate is so high. If we did a better job selecting our friends and spouses then we would not have as many relationship problems.

In my study of great people, I have found that they also knew they needed mentoring. One of the major problems in the larger African American community is the lack of cross-generational communication. In the African tradition elders are the most respected. We have too many elders in our community who are not being listened to and respected. We have young people talking back to elders and not receiving their pearls of wisdom. We have many elders who do not initiate conversations with young people, but instead want to lecture young people without listening to their concerns.

Students need to be aware that mentors may be busy and have demanding schedules. Your relationship with that person should not be so demanding that it becomes a liability to your mentor. Sometimes you need to be in your mentor's presence while he or she is talking to other people and benefit from that experience.

Habits and Discipline

One of the major problems I have observed among African American college students is that the majority of them do not have mentors. It is very difficult to become anything that you have not seen. White young men have benefited greatly in the corporate world with mentors.

Accomplished African American adults need to remember to whom much is given, much is required. They also need to emulate the White mentoring experience and build institutions. Maybe one reason why mentoring is not as strong in our communities is because we have not built institutions. Mentoring is crucial if there is a need to preserve something. While we may not have as many institutions, we have a rich history and promising future that needs nurturing. I'm appealing to both mentors and mentees to reach out to each other.

I believe good habits are essential to a successful college experience. One of the most profound quotations I have ever read provides the essence of this chapter:

"I am your constant companion. I am your greatest helper or heaviest burden. I will push you onward or drag you down to failure. I am completely at your command. Half the things you do might just as well turn over to me and I will be able to do them quickly and correctly. I am easily managed – you must merely be firm with me. Show me exactly how you want something done and after a few lessons I will do it automatically. I am the servant of all great men; and alas, of all failures, as well. Those who are great, I have made great. Those who are failures, I have made failures. I am not a machine, though I work with all the precision of a machine plus the intelligence of a man. You may run me for profit or run me for ruin – it makes no difference to me. Take me, train me, be firm with me, and I will place the world at your feet. Be easy with me and I will destroy you. Who am I? I am habit!"

Anonymous

This has been the driving force of my life. I have observed great people, and they have great habits. When Earl Graves, publisher of Black Enterprise, came to our bookstore for a booksigning, he was on a world wind tour. Earl Graves is in his 60s. He told me that the next morning he had to fly to Los Angeles. He was leaving his hotel room at 5:30a.m. for a 7a.m. flight. He was told by the hotel staff that the health club did not open until 6a.m., which was after he was scheduled to depart. He negotiated with the hotel staff to open it up early because he needed to exercise. He told me that it is not that he *wanted* to exercise but after a taxing day and before a demanding morning, he *needed* to exercise to operate at maximum efficiency. Earl Graves is successful because he has good habits.

Let's review the quotation, "Those who are great I have made great. Those who are failures I have made failures. Take me, train me, be firm with me, and I will place the world at your feet. Be easy with me and I will destroy you." I am frightened by that kind of statement as I see the attitude of African American college students chilling in the Student Union; I need a break; 15 hours is too much; the classes are too hard; the teacher doesn't like me; I'm too tired to study; but not too tired to play cards; I'm too tired to read, but not too tired to listen to rap. These are habits and the quotation reads "Be easy with me and I will destroy you." Some students are being destroyed not by White supremacy – but their bad habits.

I asked some of my friends, relatives, and mentors to give me some quotations I could share with you that have made them successful. My father's quotation was *"Did you do your best?"* When I was younger I would say "I did okay" or "I did good." He would look at me and say, "Son, I didn't ask you that." *Good* and *okay* are *best's* worst enemy. Let me now ask the reader, Did you do your best?

My track coach, Gerald Richards, used to ask me, *"Can you run when you're tired?* Anybody can run when they are fresh. The difference between winners and losers boils down to the latter part of the race when both are tired." He had us run from 3p.m. until 6p.m. and when he knew we were tired, he would announce, "Now the workout will begin." Anyone can run when they're fresh. Now I will find out if you can run when you're tired. To this day I remember that question. I use it in February with my exhausting speaking schedule. I use it throughout the year when I get tired. I still ask myself "Can you run? Can you study? Can you speak? Can you work? Can you perform when you're tired?" That's the difference between winners and losers.

Julius Irving said, "*Defeat will make you stronger.*" He reminds us about Abraham Lincoln who was defeated numerous times and became bankrupt before winning the presidency, and Thomas Edison who failed more than 300 times in his pursuit of electricity and the light bulb, and George Washington Carver who failed hundreds of times as he created 300 products from crops. Losers give up when defeated, but winners use defeat to make them stronger.

Michael Jordan reminds us "*I'm not afraid to fail.*" He did not make his high school freshmen basketball team. He worked hard in the off-season and tried again as a sophomore and made the team. Suppose Jordan had given up. Can you imagine the best NBA player to ever play did not make his freshmen team? True to his motto, he retires from basketball and tries two sports, baseball and golf, where he is less talented. Michael Jordan will try anything because he's not afraid to fail.

In my book, *To Be Popular or Smart: The Black Peer Group*, I described how many African American students who have placed themselves in a "box." Many African American students will only try out for certain extra-curricular activities because they feel those are acceptable by their peer group. How unfortunate that we feel it's not Black to be a member of the German club, Biology club, or the debate team. We need to listen to Michael Jordan. Try everything and don't be afraid to fail.

Oprah Winfrey has shared many times people come to her saying, "I would like to be a journalist, an actor, a computer programmer, a doctor, or an engineer." Oprah then says, "What's holding you back? If this is what you want to do, *just do it*." If you want to be a journalist, write. If you want to be an engineer or a doctor, study science. If you want to be an actor, act.

Maya Angelou says, "*You're worth more than that.*" Can you imagine having a personal conversation with Maya Angelou about your fears and inadequacies, and she looks at you with those wisdom filled eyes and says, "You're worth more than that? You don't need to compromise in that relationship. You don't need to be in that environment. You don't need to be treated that way. You're worth more than that."

The last quotation comes from my friend Les Brown in his book "*It's Not Over Until You Win.*" He shares the story about him and his son. They were playing a video game and Les was winning. Les said he was going to bed. His son looked at him and said, "Remember dad, It's not over until I win." Les looked at him, smiled and said, "I'm not going to let you beat me." His son looked right back with great intensity and said, "I don't expect for you to. Let's just play." Les continued to win, but finally his son won and then he looked at him and said, "Dad, now you can go to bed because remember, 'it's not over until I win.'"

Before concluding this chapter, the other major factor I have observed among great people has been their attitude.

Attitude

"The longer I live, the more I realize the impact of attitude on life. Attitude, to me, is more important than facts. It is more important than the past, than education, than money, than circumstances, than failures, than successes, than what other people think or say or do. It is more important than appearance, giftedness, or skill. It will make or break a company . . . a church . . . a home. The remarkable thing is we have a choice everyday regarding the attitude we'll embrace for that day. We cannot change our pasts . . . we cannot change the fact that people will act in a certain way. We cannot change the inevitable. The only thing we can do is play on the one string we have; and that is our attitude. I am convinced that life is 10 percent what happens to me and 90 percent how I react to it."

Anonymous

This powerful quotation reminds me of Magic Johnson. His 10 percent was being diagnosed with HIV, his 90 percent was his response. He continued to play basketball, became a spokesperson for AIDS, and built movie theatres in the inner city.

I'm reminded of Ben Carson. His 10 percent was failing fourth grade, living in a low-income neighborhood, without a father, and an illiterate mother. The 90 percent was his mother almost eliminating television and having Ben read a book and write a report weekly. He is now considered one of the world's best neurosurgeons.

I am reminded of Bo Jackson who supposedly had a career-ending injury. They said he would never play again, but because of his positive attitude, he worked hard in the off-season and continued to play baseball.

In closing, is my formula for success:

$$G + T + A + E + H + C = S.$$

God + Time + Attitude + Education + Habits + Culture = Success. With that formula let's now look at the next chapter on "Retention" and improve its present abysmal rate of 32 percent.

CHAPTER FOUR

Retention

One of the major reasons why I wrote this book was because I am very disappointed that the African American college retention rate is below 40 percent. At many colleges where I have spoken, the retention rate is closer to 25 percent. I mentioned earlier that many universities seem to have a revolving door policy. They average 1,000 African American students a semester, but they are not the same 1,000 from one semester to another. Even if a college has a retention rate of 40 percent, over half of the population is changing on a regular basis.

There have been numerous conferences to discuss retention. The retention rate is 63 percent for Asians, 56 percent for Whites, 41 percent for Latinos, and 32 percent for African Americans. The discussion of retention can become very complex and the numbers need extrapolation. Some research shows the African American retention rate as low as 25 percent and as high as 40 percent.[1] One of the first dilemmas in measuring retention is over what time period What percentage of African American freshmen graduate four years later? Five years? Six years? Many departments especially engineering have designed the curriculum so that students will not matriculate through the program in less than five years. This is due to prerequisites and courses being unavailable when students desire taking them. I've seen departments design majors where certain required courses are only offered at selected times during the year. Many students return for a fifth year for one course that for some strange reason was unavailable the second semester of the fourth year.

Universities are businesses. It took me a while to fully comprehend this. As a student, I thought colleges were only great halls of higher learning. I realized later there is also a strong economic incentive to disallow students to transfer their classes from a previous school. It's not because they don't value the courses, but because they want to earn the maximum money possible from each student.

Most statisticians have decided the best way to measure retention is over a five-year period. Some colleges that want to improve their image have chosen six years. There are some students unfortunately who have made college a career and have been enrolled for close to a decade. In a subsequent chapter on male/female relationships, we will look at the dynamic "career students" who are now 25 to 30 years of age on the same campus with 18-year-olds.

The analysis of retention is complicated because students leave and enter for a myriad of reasons. If a university wanted to measure retention in the strictest sense, they could only look at the percentage of freshmen who graduated four to five years later. That figure would be different from the percentage of students who graduated because the second number would also include transfer students. At many universities, a significant percentage of their graduates did not come from their freshmen class, but were transfer students.

When I think about retention, my major interest is not measuring the effectiveness of the university as much as trying to assess the matriculation of African American students. My focus is on what percentage of African American students attending four year colleges graduated? Notice this question does not account for students attending junior colleges nor does it address whether they transferred from Harvard to Howard. Did the student graduate and how long did it take?

I would encourage all readers to study the excellent reports released annually in *Black Issues in Higher Education* on retention and the top 100 producers of African American graduates. Again, I'm concerned how numbers are portrayed. While it seems impressive that Howard University and Florida A&M are in a continual battle on who is going to produce the most African American graduates.

Consider a university which has 10,000 African American students. Let's say they rank number one because they graduated 1,000. The truth is that only 40 percent of the freshmen class of 2,500 graduated in five years. Consider another school but much smaller has only 100 African American students and they graduated twenty which represents 80 percent of the freshmen class five years ago. The percentage of students graduating is more significant than the aggregate numbers in measuring the efficacy of the university.

In one of my earlier books *Countering the Conspiracy to Destroy Black Boys Volume IV,* I devoted an entire chapter to the difference in the graduation rate between African American males and females on campuses. While the national average for African American students hovers near 40 percent, the graduation rate for African American females nears 50 percent while the graduation rate for African American males is closer to 33 percent.[2] I am very concerned about this 17 percent differential and all of it cannot be blamed on racism.

I cited an example of an African American male and African American female, both of whom attended a Black college. Is there more racism toward the Black male at Hampton or Howard than is directed toward the female? Are there other factors? Do African American females study more than African American males? Are African American females more responsible? Are African American females more focused? Do they set clearer objectives?

Retention

Do African American males spend more time on their social life? Do African American males get "high" more than African American females? Are African American males more involved in "Greek" life? Are African American males more involved in athletics, both intercollegiate and intramural? Or is it because some mothers raise their daughters and love their sons?

There is also a retention difference between athletes and non-athletes. Surprisingly to some, the retention rate is actually greater for athletes than for non-athletes. The retention rate for athletes is closer to 50 percent.[3] There are two major reasons. One of the major factors that affects African American students matriculating is the lack of financial resources. It is an incorrect assumption to believe that the only reason African American students do not graduate is because of academics. For many African American students they did not enroll in college or complete their higher education because of a lack of financial resources.

There are some universities that even design their financial aid package where there is a declining award given for each year. There is an assumption in White America that as you matriculate through college your earning power will increase. While this may be true in the White community with a strong business climate, lucrative internships. Some White students work in their parents firms, and because of the buddy-buddy network system are able to secure summer employment making $8 to $15 an hour doing construction and other jobs. In contrast, many African American college students return to the same jobs they had in high school at McDonald's and department chain stores, if they can find employment at all!

One of the major benefits of being an athlete is that the scholarship money will be available for a minimum of four years. I mentioned earlier about the slave-type conditions that exist for many student athletes where they are required to spend between four to 10 hours daily practicing their sport. If we had to divide their annual financial aid package by the number of hours they were training you would understand why I call it slave wages. It's far less than minimum wage. This may also be the major rationale for them declaring themselves a hardship case and seeking to play on the professional level because of collegiate exploitation.

For those student athletes that choose to remain for a myriad of reasons – the nature of their sport, their level of ability, their desire to complete their education. For most of them, athletics has at least insured them a stable four-year package. I must mention that these athletes are very much aware that they must produce on a regular basis in order for their financial aid package to remain secure. That non-withstanding, one of the major elements affecting retention is the lack of financial resources for the average African American student.

Another factor that I think has helped student athletes considerably is a greater number of role models and mentors. All of us need mentoring from elementary school to the corporate boardroom. One of the major reasons Black colleges have a greater retention overall and place a greater percentage of African American students in graduate school than White colleges is because there are a greater number of African American role models on Black campuses. There are some White universities that have a 10 percent African American student population, but less than three percent African American faculty. In many athletic departments in Black or White schools, while the head coach may be White, there are numerous African American assistant coaches along with more African American upper classmen who mentor to underclassmen.

In the non-athletic African American student population, an entering freshman may have very little access to the few African American seniors scheduled to graduate. In contrast, the entering African American student athlete will have a much larger pool of African American seniors to go to for direction. I believe this is significant. Across the whole college sports picture, there is a greater graduation rate for student athletes involved in sports with less money-making potential such as track, wrestling, swimming, volleyball, golf, tennis, and gymnastics than those who play football, basketball, and baseball.

There is also a wide variance in the graduation rate of athletes at the 2,000 four-year colleges in the nation. *Black Issues in Higher Education* releases an annual report comparing the retention rates of these schools and provides an excellent analysis. Schools such as the University of Houston and Kansas State University have horrendous records of not graduating African American student athletes. In contrast, Georgetown's basketball program and Penn State's football program boast upwards of 80 percent retention. It is imperative that athletes consider these factors before they sign.

I commend former coach John Thompson at Georgetown for realizing that athletes like Patrick Ewing and Alonzo Mourning bring millions of dollars to the university and additional television coverage, while they only cost Georgetown $20,000 a year or $80,000 for a four year scholarship. That is a very good return on their investment. John Thompson and similar coaches have taken the position that the least they could do is provide a fifth year of financial eligibility, tutors, and counseling.

In the last chapter, I mentioned the impact freshmen's grades have on the overall GPA just like bowling. If you only bowled 100 in the first game, but bowled a 200 in the second, the overall average would only be 150. Many progressive universities realize that the adjustment to college life is traumatic and can be a culture shock for many students, especially students of color.

Therefore, they have designed pre-enrollment summer intensive classes ranging from two to five weeks where students can become acclimated to college life. I like these programs because they offer college courses and allow new students to adjust to the food and other cultural issues. There are few students on campus and therefore fewer distractions. I think it is a great opportunity to develop discipline and good study habits.

While every school has a new student orientation, they vary from two hours to ten days. I've had the privilege of speaking at the orientation for Morehouse College, which I consider to be one of the best. The orientation lasts 10 days preparing students academically, socially, and emphasis is placed on their political responsibility to the larger community. Spelman's orientation is similar and both culminate into a joint candle light dinner for the two schools. Many schools realize the importance of orientations. Some of the best for African Americans at White schools include Boston College, University of Georgia, Georgia Tech, Virginia Commonwealth, and West Virginia University.[3]

Unfortunately, many universities have converted the summer and freshmen year into the 13th grade, to provide remedial courses for entering college students. This is a major reason most universities estimate it will take five years to graduate students with academic deficiencies.

Many universities and junior colleges offer basic classes that do not earn college credit in reading, math and English. While all college students possess a high school diploma, and some may possess a GPA that exceeds 3.0, colleges still rely on standardized testing to determine the placement of their students. Just as high schools receive students who are reading and computing at the third grade level, colleges are admitting students who possess less than 12th grade proficiencies in reading and math.

Some universities are better than others at providing remedial courses. One of the strengths of Black colleges is their ability to accept students where they are, provide the necessary academic enrichment, and produce scholars who complete graduate studies at elite universities.

There are thousands of African American students who represent that description. I must say to K-12 grade teachers and parents who allow "social promotion" they do students a great disservice. Students think they "got over" because they are in high school possessing less than ninth grade proficiencies in reading and math. Parents either are unaware or do not care to hold themselves, their child, and the school accountable.

I spoke at an elementary school graduation where many parents were furious because the school district decided not to graduate a child that was not on grade level. They should have been furious at their children, teachers, and themselves before the graduation ceremony, and not at the district office.

Colleges do not have to accept students with less than a 12th grade reading and math level. Some colleges have a mission to develop African American students and they have chosen to teach "13th grade" students. Some are financially driven and have concluded it is a lucrative decision to prolong graduation a couple years. What are some colleges to do if they have 4,000 slots available and only have 4,000 applicants and 500 of those applicants had a subpar high school performance?

My major concern is about African American students who think they got over and did not earn their high school diploma. They will take remedial courses at college cost. It would have been cheaper to master this information free during K-12 grade. This is a major justification for junior colleges. It is expensive taking remedial courses at $10,000 a year at a four-year college with room and board when junior colleges can perform the same task for less than a $1,000 per year.

Over the past two decades that I have been speaking on college campuses, I have tried to share with students strategies that can improve their ability to graduate in a timely manner from college. The following are those strategies.

ATTENDING CLASS

This may sound so simple but for some strange reason many African American students, just like the larger population, don't attend class. They are paying $15,000 per year for 15 class hours per week and yet have found other priorities over attending class. I often tease students, especially when the college is in a rural area, "What do you have better to do in this town than to go to class?"

Many students feel they have some very legitimate alternatives: I didn't go to class because I was sleepy. My hair needed braiding. The professor is boring. The test is based on the book and not the lecture. My friends will give me their notes or the cassette. It was too far to walk. It was too cold. Too hot. It was raining. I just didn't feel like going. The professor doesn't take attendance. I don't like being in a class where I am the only African American student.

These are just some of the many excuses I've heard for poor attendance. I have tried to share with students that even if you sleep in class there is a possibility that you could hear something that you could use on the final exam. *I don't believe there is a better place on campus than in class.* Something is wrong when African American students prefer the Student Union, gymnasium, cafeteria, or kicking it with their friends in the dormitory more than the classroom.

C LASS P ARTICIPATION

Another strategy that African Americans could use to improve retention is class participation. When your grade could go either direction, professors consider class participation, seat selection, and your interaction with them. Many failing students never speak in class, sit in the rear, and have never talked with the professor.

S TUDY S KILLS

Many African American students are not aware that there is a difference between homework, cramming, and studying. Many African American college students do not possess good study skills. They know how to do homework, but were never taught how to study. At some high schools many teachers have stopped giving homework since 50 percent or less of the class was not completing the assignments, it became difficult to discuss homework the following day.

Operating on the premise that African American students in college know how to do homework, the challenge is learning study skills. Many African American students lack internal discipline but respond well to external stimuli. Many African American students would rather complete problems 1-10 than voluntarily reading a chapter in preparation for a class discussion.

Students with poor study habits do not do well when teachers give pop quizzes. A student who is current with the reading material not only is prepared for class discussion, but is equally prepared for a surprise quiz or test.

The first objective in reading the chapter is to become familiar with the content. Secondly, you should outline the chapter. Third, answer the questions at the end of the chapter. If there is difficulty in any of the above stages you should read the chapter again. Any words in the chapter that you did not understood should be looked up in a dictionary immediately. People with good study habits keep a notepad to jot down unfamiliar words that can be looked up later. Ultimately, after reviewing the chapter using aforementioned ideas, a good student should be able to write a summary of the chapter.

When I was a college student majoring in economics, I used to quiz myself on the material by acting as if I were the professor, teaching the class. It is a humbling experience when you think you have mastered the information, only to realize when you stand before the class you are deficient. Oftentimes, concepts I thought I understood I had to review in the book before continuing my mock lecture. This practice prepared me for class discussions and tests.

There are primarily two ways information is disseminated in college: textbook and lecture. I've observed many students in a lecture hall listening but not taking notes. Some students take inadequate notes. They write down 10 words from an hour lecture. Better note takers write five pages of notes from the same lecture. Students with good study habits allocate time to review the lecture notes and rewrite them shortly after class.

Students are taking a major chance if they assume an entire test will be based on the book. Let's say there are five questions on the final exam, and four from the textbook, the remaining question came from the lecture notes. If you mastered the book, at best, you would only receive an 80 which in most schools will only give you a C. The only way to earn an A or B would have been to equally master the material presented in the lecture.

Just as we have made a distinction between studying and doing homework, some African American students also don't understand the distinction between studying and cramming. A person with good study habits has consistently over the course of the class been reading the chapters in advance and taking good lecture notes.

Many African American students wait until the last week of the class to cram. Some cram the night before the final exam. They attempt to digest 16 chapters and notes between noon and midnight. They attempt to convince themselves, friends, and parents that they studied hard. You can't compare someone who studied 12 hours in succession with someone who studied four hours daily throughout the semester.

I won't even discuss how sleepy crammers are when they enter class to take the final exam. I have observed that students with good study habits have to do very little the day before the final exam. This is a very good barometer of good study habits. Those students who have poor study habits spend an inordinate amount of time studying the day before the exam. Students with better study habits will have an even distribution throughout the semester. This not only will provide them with more sleep the night before the final exam, but less stress as well. I can't even begin to imagine the negative impact that lack of sleep, stress, and cramming has on the grades of students with poor study habits.

T IME O N T ASK

I believe life is very simple. *Whatever you do most will be what you do best.* I don't believe Shockley, Jensen, or Charles Murray that Africans are genetically inferior. I don't believe African Americans score less than other students on standardized tests because we are inferior. I don't believe the reason African Americans are 88 percent of the NBA starters is because we are genetically superior.

What I observe is that in the African American community, we play basketball until we can't see the hoop. I witness more African American college students in the union than in the library. There are some libraries that have become so social clubs that many students have to find other places to study.

In high school, Asian students study 12 hours a week, White students 8 hours a week and African Americans only 5 hours a week. The research also shows that we spend 30 hours watching television, 18 hours listening to music, 11 hours on the telephone, and 9 hours playing outside.[5] The sad commentary is that these figures may not be much different among college students. I often ask college students, "Do you study more than you watch television? Do you study more than you listen to rap? Talk on the telephone? Party? Do you study more than you hang out in the Student Union or the cafeteria? Do you study more than you get high? Do you study more than you spend time with your fraternity or sorority? Do you study more than you play cards?" I even ask some students, "Do you study more than you have sex?" More will be said about that in the chapter on male/female relationships.

I believe our retention rate of 32 percent could be increased if we simply increased our study time. Some students having academic problems think if they don't party they could increase their study time. Staying away from the party is not synonymous with studying. Unfortunately, for many students partying involves not only the actual hours of the party, but getting high prior to the party and recovering from it afterwards. A four hour party could affect much of the prior evening and the following morning. I was disciplined enough to attend the party and by 9a.m. I was back into the books. Maybe some students are aware of their personality and have to eliminate partying completely regardless of whether they are actually studying during the party.

STUDYING TOGETHER

African American college students seem to do everything together but study. They play ball together, pledge together, get high together, party together, eat together, make love together, have fun together, but don't study together. If you look at the Asian community not only do they study more than any other population, but they also study together. I've also observed this among White students especially in the math and science courses, particularly calculus, statistics, chemistry, and physics.

There are a myriad of reasons why African American students don't study together. Some have had the unfortunate experience of being in a group of four where one or more members did not equally bring their resources to the table. Cooperative learning or studying together is different from students taking advantage of better students. Studying together is based on the premise that each student will carry their load.

The ideal structure of studying together would be preparing for a test on four chapters where each student is responsible to present the information on a particular chapter and quiz the others. Anyone who violates the rule "equal participation for equal benefits" should be warned and ultimately removed from the group for non-compliance. Some students act like parasites and many of our better students don't hold each other accountable.

Another major reason why we don't study together is that we have not been taught. At many African American elementary and high schools cooperative learning is not encouraged. Teachers use a dictatorial pedagogy. Another factor that could contribute to the lack of studying together is that the more advanced African American students, the creme de la creme, do not have a need to study with anyone else. Many of them are in for a rude awakening when an A at their school translates into a C at another school.

Some African American students attended integrated high schools. They were some of the few African American students in AP and honors classes. Due to racism that existed within the class, some were not invited to be part of a study group. Others were invited to be part of the multiracial study group. Because they took an oath of "blackness" they were required not to take an AP or honors class, or if they did take it, never be seen associating with White and Asian students after class, in the library, or visiting each other in a study group. They are in a very complex situation because they are in a multiracial class of higher achieving students who have been taught the value studying together and yet because of their oath of blackness they are having to compete against others without the benefit of group study. The sad reality is that this oath of blackness sometimes exists on the college campus.

T UTORING

My definition of someone who is educated is one who knows *what* it is he does not know and knows *where* to go to find it. Many African American students, especially males because of a large insecure ego, do not want to admit they need tutoring.

I have met numerous African American students who failed a course because they would not admit to themselves they needed tutorial. Most universities provide free tutorial services. Why a student for egotistical reasons would decline tutoring and face the consequence of failing the class is beyond me. Many universities have become sensitive to this dilemma and have provided tutors within the student's own race hoping that race would not be a hindering factor.

Students should accept the fact that they do not know everything or they would not be in college. If they knew the material they would not need a professor or textbook. Therefore, if you need a professor and a textbook then why not acknowledge you may need a tutor? You may also be pleasantly surprised when you go into the tutorial assistance center and find White and Asian students taking advantage of the resource as well.

America is a test taking country geared toward left-brain thinkers. Consequently, all of us have to be prepared to master test taking. Until such time that we can convince educators that standardized tests don't predict successful outcomes and that there are other ways to measure learning other than culturally bias, middle class questions on ditto sheets, true/false, multiple choice exams. Unfortunately, tests are the gatekeeper to AP, honors, gifted and talented classes, magnet schools, colleges, course selection, graduate and professional school. Many colleges require their potential graduates to pass an exit exam. I have met college students who possess an excellent GPA and have taken all required classes, but were denied graduation until they passed exit exams. Many professions including medical, dental, law, accounting, teaching, nursing, and numerous other professions require an exit exam.

Retention

Many industries require periodically throughout your career additional tests to maintain your license. African Americans may be the least prepared group to take the most important test of our lives that will determine our career, income, and standard of living. Other groups secure copies of the tests legally and some illegally. I am not condoning cheating nor illegally securing the tests. There are workbooks, software, and courses available for the IOWA, California, Metropolitan, ACT, SAT, GRE, GMAT, and many other tests. College students can ask their professor for a sample test given in prior semesters.

There are several areas of test taking that we need to review. Obviously the most important area of test taking is having an adequate understanding of the information. There is no substitute for knowledge and studying not cramming is the most effective way to acquire the information.

Unfortunately not only is America a test taking country, but success is based on test taking speed. In the real world, the corporate community, and in the game of life, decisions are not always based on speed but on accuracy. Why Americans thinks that someone is smarter than another because they can answer one hundred questions in one hundred minutes is beyond logic. Sometimes I have delayed a decision for several days because I wanted to ponder all ramifications before making a final decision. I wonder how many African American students have choked under the time constraint of a test and done poorly. I wonder how many African American students place the correct answer in the wrong box in their haste. We must learn how to relax while taking tests. This will only happen with mastery of the content and practicing under test-taking conditions.

When I was in college, I determined that schools valued grades more than they valued learning. The test determined the grade. I decided to play the game and reverse the role and became the teacher. Several days before the final exam, I would close my notebook and textbook and develop my own questions. To construct a question is to know the answer in reverse. My objective was to make my exam more challenging than the professor. It is encouraging to realize my exams were more rigorous.

This strategy works excellently for a disciplined student, but if you gave yourself an easy "Mickey Mouse" test the night before the final exam then you were ill prepared. It is unfair to blame the professor if you felt the test was too rigorous when the questions came from the same sources to which you had access.

Retention

P RAYER A ND S CRIPTURE

Lastly, they can never take prayer out of school as long as you are saved. I believe you should never take a test without praying to God for wisdom. You need to recall those scriptures "I can do all things through Christ who strengthens me. I shall look to the hills. Where does my help come from? My help cometh from the Lord. Remember, you have not because you ask not." The Word reminds us, "I will bless you exceedingly, abundantly, beyond what you could ever ask or think."

And now we enter the final exam. First, you should scan the entire test not only to compare your final exam to theirs, but also to give you some idea of the nature of the questions and the amount of time you should allocate to each section.

Second, you should answer questions in the order of least difficulty. All questions that you know the answer readily should be answered first. Be very careful to place your answers in the appropriate box. Many students test poorly because they place their answers in the wrong box. This is the downside of answering questions out of sequence. Many students do poorly because they don't properly read the directions. Some students forget to place their names on the final exam. This has delayed them from receiving their results, especially when other students made the same mistake.

There are usually three types of exam questions – true/false, multiple choice, and essay. Some students have told me they prefer essay questions because they can write endlessly. If you understand the nature of the test, reverse the roles and if you were the professor what ideas would you be looking for in the answer? I have seen students answer one essay question with a three page answer that did not include any of the major points the professor was seeking. If the points are hidden and buried within the three pages, many times professors may overlook them because they have so many papers to evaluate. Students need to think like the professor not only in the pre-exam stage, but also in the post-exam stage.

The best way to answer an essay question is to provide the major points at the outset and then develop them. The reality is a student who only wrote one paragraph and mentioned the major points will receive a higher score than a student who wrote three pages who either never mentioned the major points or buried them within the paper.

Some students prefer true/false over multiple choice because they have at least a 50 percent chance of success while with multiple choice they only have a 25 percent chance. My concern is that both of these percentages are failing. We need to increase the odds.

To successfully answer true/false questions you need to read the entire question. Many students make the mistake of answering the question as being true because they read the first part of the question which was true, but the remainder of the question was false. If that is the case then the entire question is false. When a question uses words like *always, never, must,* and *all,* more times than not those questions or statements are false. Questions or statements where there are qualifying words like *sometimes, normally, often,* and *generally,* create a greater chance of being true.

Sometimes true/false questions can be tricky because they are very long. The secret in answering these questions is first to find out what exactly are they asking. There could literally be six areas of this question or statement. There is only one relevant sentence to be determined true or false. That is the only one you need to answer. When time begins to expire and you have exhausted your understanding of the questions then and only then do you resort to the 50/50 chance and guess. This should be the option of last resort.

The last area of test taking is multiple choice. I wonder how many students have taken a multiple choice test and after reading the four answers became so thoroughly confused that while originally they knew the correct answer they ultimately chose an incorrect answer.

One of the most effective techniques in multiple choice exams is to read the question thoroughly and ask yourself what exactly is the question asking. Many times the question is very long and confusing. Once you have identified the question you should think of the correct answer and look for that answer.

It is imperative that you read all four answers. Most tests are designed where the first answer is the closest answer to being correct but has the least probability. Answers further down oftentimes encompass answer one with terminology such as *some of the above* or *all of the above*. Many students who chose the first answer were not aware that answers three and four contained them.

While multiple choice only offers you a 25 percent probability this can be improved to at least 50 percent by using the process of elimination. In most multiple choice exams while answer one is the closest to being correct with the least probability, there are normally two answers with very little probability and often one of them borders on being ludicrous. Therefore, a good test taker can use the process of elimination for two answers, and guess between the two remaining.

Mastering test taking skills is essential in graduating from college. Retention can be enhanced with a relationship between student and advisor. Many students spend a fifth or sixth year in college because they had poor academic advisement. When I was in college I knew I needed 128 credits to graduate. I knew I needed 30 hours in my major. I kept a score card at the end of each year checking off the requirements of liberal arts and my major. My advisor told me that if I made the mistake of planning to take a course when I desired versus when it is offered, I might increase the risk of delaying graduation.

It is unfortunate for any student to have to return to college for one or two courses. I'm also critical of universities that design their courses in such a way that even when students are monitoring their progress in a very deliberate fashion, they are unsuccessful at graduating in four years. I mentioned earlier that universities are like businesses. Unfortunately some colleges are more callous than others. I'm equally concerned about the wide variance in the GPA requirements among various departments within the same university. There are universities, specifically along the eastern sea board, where some departments require greater than a 3.0 to be admitted. They literally want to admit honor roll students before admission. There are departments that increase the requirements of the GPA because of their gatekeeping, classist, elitist mindset. They only want a certain number in their particular field.

I have observed students who were unable to meet departmental requirements and ultimately had to graduate with a degree in general studies. They successfully satisfied the university's requirements for graduation with a 2.0 but were unable to be admitted into a department that had a standard greater than 2.0.

A student who had a poor freshman year would have a very difficult time being admitted into certain departments that require a 3.0 GPA. Can you imagine your career being derailed because of a departmental requirement that you are unable to achieve? I wonder how many doctors, lawyers, engineers, accountants, and computer programmers have we lost due to departments' GPA requirements? Students should assess the school and departments before enrolling.

I wish that university administrators would thoroughly review their curriculum to confirm that students can graduate in four years. The National Retention Project under the leadership of Dr. Clinita Ford has over 284 universities who are committed to retention of African American students. Their research of successful programs delineates that commitment must come from the president's office, but commitment without proper funding is counterfeit. Two decades ago the financial aid packages consisted of two-thirds grants, but now there are one-half loans. Many African American students are not academic dropouts, but withdraw due to finances. Retention programs must provide comprehensive services including tutorial, academic advisement, personal counseling, mentoring, sensitizing faculty, marketing the program to avoid stigmatization, providing religious expression, and cultural outlets which may include an African American house.[6]

If I were an African American professor teaching a course in African American studies and there were White students who also took my course, I would be disappointed if White students received a higher grade in my class than African American students. That actually happens. While some people are critical of author and Professor Shelby Steele and some of his ideas this scenario has happened to him. It did not happen because African American students are genetically inferior. It did not occur because he had higher expectations of White students or gave them a better grade. It occurred because some African American students thought the class would be easy. They did not read the book or listen to the lecture because they were going to rap their way to an A, talking about their personal experiences. I have observed African American students incensed, irritated, and intimidated by White students who had read the material and were able to participate fully in classroom discussions.

Just as I think it is embarrassing for a high school to be predominately Black and Latino and yet White and Asian students constitute the majority of AP, honors, and gifted students this is equally appalling. Where is the pride? Where is the standard of excellence? I also believe it is unadulterated gall for African American students after class to say to the African American professor, "Come on brother," "Come on sister," "Why don't you help me out and give me a grade?" If the African American professor does not favorably respond to the request, they categorize him or her as an "*Oreo*" and an "Uncle Tom." I also wonder how many African American professors want to be advisors to African American student groups after those types of experiences?

My major concern is the academic success of African American college students. The next three chapters will look at some of the social dynamics that are affecting college students. They include: Greek life, male/female relationships, and the Black college students' role in the liberation struggle of African people.

CHAPTER FIVE

Greek Life

Of all the chapters in the book, this will probably be the most challenging because of the sensitive nature of this subject. I am not going to declare in this book whether I am a member of a Greek fraternity or not. There are three major groups that will be reading this chapter. First there are members of Greek fraternities and sororities. There are approximately 1.5 million members.[1] Most of them will be very sensitive and critical of anyone making disparaging remarks about their organization.

There was an excellent article about hazing in the June 12, 1997 issue of *Black Issues in Higher Education*. The following week there was a scathing letter written by a member of the Pan Hellinic Council telling *Black Issues* that Greek life was none of their business and they should concern themselves with the academics of collegiate life.

The largest group of people who will be reading this chapter have never pledged. They have very little knowledge about pledging or the intake process and are not cognizant of the many benefits of Greek life. They are not privy to the camaraderie that exists among the members and their successful projects worldwide. They may only be familiar with hazing and the criticism of Greek life.

The third group that we will be reading about in this chapter is probably the most objective. They are inactive members who understand Greek history, philosophy, and current programs, but for a myriad of reasons (demanding schedule, disgruntled with undergraduate chapters, poor access to local progressive graduate chapters) are no longer active. Unfortunately, this will be the smallest group reading this chapter.

If I declared I was a member of a fraternity, the largest group of people reading this chapter would accuse me of not being objective and defending something I had to endure beatings to achieve. If I told you that I was not a member of a Greek fraternity then I would be accused by the 1.5 million of talking about something I know nothing about and not fully appreciating the great work being done by Greeks that the media does not cover.

If I declared I was an inactive member I would be accused of being a "Benedict Arnold." A true member remains "down with the program" and would not divulge "family business." I am a member of one of those three groups and my major desire is that you appreciate the ideas disseminated in this chapter without being prejudiced about your own membership status.

There is a long and great tradition of Greek life in Black America. In 1906, just forty-one years after slavery ended, the first African American fraternity, Alpha

Phi Alpha, was founded at Cornell University. Kappa Alpha Psi and Omega Psi Phi were founded in 1911 at Indiana University and Howard University respectively. Phi Beta Sigma was founded in 1914 also at Howard University. Iota Phi Theta was founded much later in 1963 at Morgan State University. The first African American sorority, Alpha Kappa Alpha, was founded in 1908 at Howard University. In 1913 Delta Sigma Theta was founded at the same university along with Zeta Phi Beta in 1920. Sigma Gamma Rho was founded in 1922 at Butler University.

Anyone critical of Greek life needs to look at the history and the mission of Greek life. Can you imagine being an African American male in upper state New York during the height of the lynchings of the early 1900s, attending a prestigious school like Cornell University and experiencing Jim Crow racism? Five years later the Kappas were experiencing the same stress at Indiana University and Sigma Gamma Rho Sorority in 1922 at Butler University.

I wanted to start with Greek life on White campuses because it was only after Brown vs. Topeka in 1954, the Voting Rights Act of 1964, and the Adams decision in 1973 that there were a greater number of African American students at White schools than Black colleges. Before integration most fraternities and sororities were restricted to Black colleges. Today most fraternities and sororities have over 700 chapters at Black and White universities. African American men and women were not allowed to be members of White fraternities and sororities in that era. Some would say that African Americans becoming Greek is a reaction of being denied entrance into White fraternities and sororities. They would say that Greek life is a glorification of White history and White culture. This chapter will conclude with a brief description of an Africentric fraternity. Our historical challenge has always been being African in White America. W.E.B. DuBois described it as "two warring souls within us." How much of our Greek behavior is a reaction to White supremacy and how much of our behavior is proactive of our own history and culture?

Can you imagine going to Howard University in the 1920s during the zenith of the Harlem Renaissance? Howard is the founding home of the AKAs, Omegas, Deltas, Sigmas, and Zetas. While there are 1.4 million African American students enrolled in college presently, back in the 1920s there were less than 20,000. They were the creme de la creme. Howard University was surely the place to attend. The Harlem Renaissance was a very great time in Black American history.

The major objective of African American fraternities and sororities is to aid their fellow brothers and sisters in achieving academic excellence and to ensure graduation. These fraternities and sororities did not have to be reminded by the Asians that one of the secrets to success is studying together. These fraternities and sororities were founded not only to assist each other in graduation, but also in career pursuits, employment referrals, clothing and food drives, tutorial, scholarships, and other civic causes.

All those who are critical of fraternities and sororities need to acknowledge that other than the church no other group has given more scholarships, conducted more food and clothing drives, provided more mentoring and tutorial services, fought against illiteracy, attempted to reduce teen pregnancy and taught male responsibility. Several fraternities and sororities even have housing and technical programs on the continent of Africa.

For all those critical of Greek life, to be a Black man living in Ithaca, New York attending Cornell University there was probably no better group to join than Alpha Phi Alpha. A sister in 1922 living in Indiana attending Butler University probably had no better group to join than Zeta Phi Beta.

There are many people who have been critical of the pledging process, but most of them have never pledged. If you have ever been "on line" it is not only a test of your will, but also an opportunity to work with another group of brothers and sisters where your personal success is predicated on the success of the group. During the pledging experience most lines have a minimum of seven on line, but some have been as small as two. You are quizzed, tested, badgered, and confronted by your big brothers and sisters. Every time you answer incorrectly, your fellow brother or sister is punished. Can you imagine being sent to the restroom to help your brother or sister answer correctly because if they continue to answer incorrectly, you get beat? The lesson is not only the acquisition of the information, but also that you are a team, no one is more important than anyone else, and each must hold the other accountable.

It has been said that no fraternity pledges harder than the Ques of Omega Psi Phi. I don't know if it's because they were the first Black fraternity at a Black university or if it was the nature of the original founders. It has been said that once you pledge Que you will be a Que until the day you die. Many brothers felt so intensely about the Que experience they were even branded.

I have often wondered what happens in that pledging experience that creates such loyalty that often exceeds the commitment to the race and to God. Some people are critical of Greeks for being elitist. My prayer is that Greek brothers and sisters will be as committed to the race and God as they are to their fraternity and sorority. Maybe the reason that many Greeks are more loyal to their frats and sorors is because they had to earn it and believe me when you have pledged, when you are a "made" brother or sister, you have earned it. They are a "made" brother or sister.

Most Greeks appreciate the membership and don't take for granted the work and sacrifices that were required. Many of us take being Black for granted. We don't appreciate the struggle of Paul Cuffe, Joseph Cinque, Harriet Tubman, Nat Turner, Sojourner Truth, and Denmark Vesey.

We take Jesus, His grace, salvation, and eternal life for granted. We take for granted that we have been paid for with a price and that we've been washed by the blood. We take for granted that Jesus died for us. In the pledging experience it was your blood, but on the cross it was HIS and some of us take it for granted. Maybe if we had had to walk from Mississippi to Canada with Harriet Tubman or hung on the cross at Calvary we would have a greater appreciation.

I often ask college students who desired being a member of a fraternity or a sorority, "Why did you join?" I challenge them to be honest. I don't want them to tell me they joined because of academic or civic reasons if it's a lie. I would like all readers who are Greek to be honest and ask themselves why did you join? I am not saying there were no social reasons why our brothers became Alphas at Cornell in 1906 nor for our sisters who became AKAs at Howard University. I would like to juxtapose the motives of the founders in the early 1900s with our objectives as we approach the 21st century.

Some Greeks, if they are honest, pledged because they wanted to be popular. Others pledged because of the attention they would receive during the step show. Some pledged because it gave them inroads to the opposite sex. If I am an Alpha there are opportunities for me to interact with Alpha Angels and sometimes AKAs who were not dating other brothers. If I'm a Que there are opportunities for me to interact with Omega Pearls and my sister sorority Delta Sigma Theta. If I'm a Kappa I may have greater success with a Kappa Kitten.

I described the above in very nice language. The truth is that at some schools the above is actually outright prostitution. I've seen women used as a piece of meat. I've seen misogynist, sexist behavior that was unbecoming of real men and real women.

In my freshman year we had in excess of 1,000 African American students. Many of them were jockeying to be somebody. These students were at a very critical and volatile age when they seek self-esteem from group acceptance. This really is faulty thinking because self-esteem is not based on peer acceptance.

I try to encourage students who are contemplating pledging to wait until they have secured self-esteem. It reminds me of the marriages where people who feel incomplete believe that marriage will fulfill them and make them whole people. You don't need a fraternity or sorority to be complete. Fraternities and sororities would be stronger if their membership was made of self-actualized people. On college campuses the students who receive the most respect, attention, sex and favors are athletes, Greeks, and upper class persons.

In one of my earlier books *Good Brothers Looking for Good Sisters,* I'm critical of some females who say they are looking for a good man but will overlook an intellectual, a nice guy, or a devout Christian. They want to date a 6'6" basketball player or the best Kappa stepper.

You don't have to be a nuclear physicist to learn the hierarchy and pecking order on most college campuses. Most males who are neither athletes nor Greeks will receive less attention from African American females. It would take a very secure African American male to consciously decide not to pledge or become a ballplayer, concentrate on his studies, join the Black Student Union, and participate in a Bible study group. Unfortunately you receive more attention when you step at the party than when your steps are ordered by the Lord.

Some of the major issues affecting Greeks in campus life are pledging, hazing, the intake process, and the lack of unity. I mentioned earlier the pledging process was designed not only to test your acquisition of information, but to measure your will power and your team spirit. Unfortunately, over the years pledging has grown into hazing and some members have been maimed and some have even died.

Imagine being a parent, who sends your son (or daughter) off to college. You feel a sense of accomplishment because you have raised your child in the inner city and he has survived safely. Now you're sending him/her off to college in a rural environment with other college students to engage each other intellectually. You are optimistic that your child will return with a college degree. Imagine how you would feel when you're called late at night by the university hospital and informed that your son or daughter died being hazed?

I wonder what the Black Greek founders at Cornell, Indiana University, and Howard are thinking now? Is this what it was all about? Did they intend on sending DuBois' Talented Tenth off to college where they could be killed not by the KKK but by the Kappas? There have been horror stories over the past decade involving both male and female, even though it has been worse for males. The females have been orally abused and physically beat. Some of our males have died.

My first concern is what happens to the GPA during the pledging experience. In White schools where there are lower standards for fraternities and sororities a person can pledge with as few as 12 hours and a GPA of only 2.0. I have seen students pledge in the second semester of their freshman year, placed on probation after pledging and never recover academically or return to the university.

At Black colleges there is a requirement of 24 hours and a GPA between 2.0 and 2.3. This at least requires you to be a sophomore who survived the tumultuous freshman experience. It does not preclude that you are mature enough to pledge the first semester of your sophomore year, but hopefully you are more mature than you were as a second semester freshman. I believe it is tragic for someone to pledge and be rewarded with probation or expulsion.

One of the historic missions of fraternities and sororities is academic excellence. Ideally speaking, becoming a member of a fraternity or sorority should improve your grades. I would challenge Greeks to act like elitist departments I described in the previous chapter and raise their academic standards. Wouldn't it be nice if we could return to the original mission of fraternities and sororities? They only admitted the best and pledging enhanced the GPA. Can you imagine a line pledging and making the honor roll? Today, some students take nine hours of sewing, basket weaving, bidwhist and roller skating while pledging.

Under normal circumstances the pledging experience lasted only seven weeks, but there have been numerous violations. Some lines have pledged for two semesters. Mike Tyson and Roberto Alomar have nothing on some of the fraternities and sororities and what they have done. I have heard of big sisters spitting in pledgees' faces. I heard one story where a big sister called her pledgees at 3a.m. during a winter snow storm to come over to her dormitory to give her a glass of water. When they arrived she decided she didn't want the water, but threw it on the pledgees. Sisters' pledging have had to wear clothing unbecoming of what their original sisters had intended at Howard University. Pledgees have been turned into maid servants, to clean, cook and massage their big sister like they were on a Georgia plantation. Sisters have been beaten and have welts to prove it.

The brothers who did not want to be outdone have gone a little further. It is one thing to paddle a brother on the buttocks, but it is another thing to beat him so badly that he has cracked ribs, a broken nose, a damaged eye, broken teeth, a ruptured spleen, or a damaged kidney or liver. I have seen brothers come back from Vietnam looking better than brothers who have been hazed. The tragedy has worsened because brothers are now dying on line.

Can you imagine your son being tied to the railroad tracks while pledging and having a heart attack before they finally let him go before the oncoming train? There have been brothers who were beaten so badly that they finally had to be taken to the hospital, but only after their big brothers stopped at McDonald's to celebrate. Shortly after arrival the hospital pronounced the pledgee dead.

The problem is systemic. This is no longer pledging or hazing, its fratricide and exists at Black and White universities nationwide. There is no region that has been exempt. We have not only lost lives, but it has become very expensive. Families have sued the university and the fraternity or sorority for upwards to a million dollars.

There are some fraternities and sororities that have been on probation for several years. I have visited some where, only 2 out of 9 Greek organizations were eligible to have people on line due to violations. It is a sad day in Greek life.

The National Panelenic Conference (NPHC) has issued the following statement on hazing:

"Hazing in any form is a violation of NPHC rules. In the event that a campus or alumni council becomes aware of any potential hazing incident it has the responsibility to immediately notify college/university administrators as well as the appropriate fraternity or sorority in which the incident is suspected. Specifically there shall be no physical, mental, or verbal abuse, scare tactics, horseplay, practical jokes or tricks, or any humiliating or demeaning acts which might negatively affect any prospective member to or during the intake process and the ceremonial ritual while becoming a member of the affiliate organizations chapter. A membership intake process has been implemented in each NPHC member organization, a process which eliminates pledging as a requirement for initiation. There are three important components in the membership intake process for NPHC affiliate organizations. Generally the process includes: 1) a pre-induction/orientation 2) the final induction ceremony 3) an in-depth education program."

This is a very strong and positive position taken by the national offices of these nine fraternities and sororities to return the integrity to the original mission. How did it become so bad? What happened between 1906 and the year 2000? Did hazing occur because each line wanted to induce greater abuse than that which was afflicted upon them? Fraternities and sororities are guilty of the same disease that White supremacists have, and that is the desire to control and have power over someone else. Did hazing occur because fraternities and sororities operate like the military which believes it has to break a person down before it makes them?

Greek Life

Did hazing occur because, as I mentioned in an earlier chapter we no longer have "DuBois' Talented Tenth." Instead, we have a large number of students who are in the 13th grade with reading and math scores below collegiate standards. Did hazing occur because today's youth are mesmerized and inculcated with the lyrics and values of gangster rap? Are fraternities and sororities becoming a mirror image of gangs? Did hazing occur because as we achieved integration and increased the number of chapters to upwards of 700 that it became difficult, if not impossible, for the national office to monitor? Is hazing occurring off campus where it is almost impossible for graduate students and alumni to monitor?

These are very challenging times for Greek life. Everyone seems to have their own opinion of how these issues need to be handled. I hope and pray that everyone agrees that no one should die or be maimed during the pledging process. I would like to believe that we all agree that a pledgee's GPA should increase during the process. Unfortunately, there is a difference of opinion among the national office, some alumni, and upperclassmen. At the national conference there is a schism between those brothers and sisters who were "made" and brothers and sisters who went through the intake process. They are often ridiculed and called "paper" brothers and sisters. There have even been incidents where brothers and sisters who went through the intake process ultimately pledged to gain acceptance.

No one wants to be a member of an organization with a two tier system. Consequently, many pledgees have expressed the desire to pledge rather than go through the paper process of intake. The national office has a tremendous challenge trying to monitor Greek activities at over 1,400 schools. It is even more difficult to monitor them when big brothers and sisters and their pledgees have gone underground and taken an oath of silence.

At many universities where there are very few African American faculty members and even fewer African American males, it becomes difficult trying to find a sponsor who will be a liaison between the fraternity and the university. Many African American faculty members would rather not be bothered defending fraternities and sororities on a weekly basis to the university because of some violation. For example, my frat brother misses my Friday morning class, but was involved in a fraternity party Friday evening that went wild. The fracas at the party included damages to university property and now I, as the sponsor, have to defend them to the university. Also, I cannot imagine being an African American faculty member where members of my fraternity are taking my class, and they assume that just because we are brothers that will earn them a grade.

On the other hand there are some of us who have a totally different experience of Greek life. We pledged honorably. It was a tremendous challenge; there were 15 on line and all 15 went over. We have remained close throughout the past two decades. When some of us were seeking employment, a referral, a letter of recommendation, or needed to secure a loan, we were able to network within our fraternity to achieve the desired outcome.

Our graduate chapter has developed a Saturday mentoring program for Black boys. We tutor, provide field trips, take them to work with us, teach them sexual responsibility and the pitfalls of drug trafficking. Last year at our annual banquet, we raised over $60,000 in scholarships and were able to give 12 aspiring young men $5,000 each in scholarships.

I have attended fraternity, civil rights, and religious conferences, and have discovered that there is more business being taken care of among fraternities and sororities than there are in civil rights and religious organizations. I am not saying that there is not a social component, but that the extent of the socializing depends on who is sponsoring the conference.

Some people see Greek life as being very divisive. Some people believe that it is a result of the Willie Lynch letter where we were taught to divide and conquer and look for differences. When my older son was attending Tuskegee University, two boys were killed. One was an

Alpha and the other was a Kappa. One was from Detroit and one was from Chicago. That's the kind of nonsense that takes place on some of our campuses. Whether the university has a student body of 20,000 and 1,000 are African American or whether it's 5,000 and almost all of them are African American students, we cannot allow ourselves to be divided into splinter groups.

As a public speaker to many universities, it is primarily the Black Student Union that brings me in. One of their major challenges has always been the support of fraternities and sororities. I have encouraged Black Student Union coordinators to try to place them on the program and maybe that might entice them to attend. How unfortunate that we now have to act like politicians to get our people to be involved in programs that will help make their lives better. In the spirit of the Million Man March we all need to remember when the police pulls us over at 3a.m. on some dead end road that they don't ask if you are an Alpha, a Que, a Kappa, or a Sigma? If they don't ask, why should we? I would like to believe that if I am a student on your campus and having problems that you will come to my aid whether I am your Greek brother or not.

It disappoints me when I am on campus to speak and fraternities and sororities schedule a meeting at the same time, or there is a party that they have sponsored and for some reason, a 10p.m. starting time precludes their attendance at my 7p.m. speech. *Greeks need to read their history because the founders would have been in attendance to hear a liberating message.* Being Greek does not exempt fraternities or sororities from their responsibilities to be committed to their race. How can a brother or sister memorize Greek history and not know their own African history? African Americans need to remember that they were African before they became Greek. Imhotep preceded Hippocrates in medicine. Ahmose preceded Pythagarus in mathematics. Aesop was African not Greek.

Greeks need to acknowledge that Africa is the origin of civilization. Some African American students have taken this challenge to heart and have developed an African fraternity called Kemet with chapters at Morehouse, Penn State, and Long Beach State, just to name a few. In Long Island New York in 1977, brothers have created Malik Sigma Psi and the sisters have founded Malika Kiambe Umfazi. While these African fraternities don't have the 100,000 members of the Greek fraternities nor 200 chapters, and access to the tremendous networking potential that exists among Greeks, they do feel well grounded in Africentricity. They celebrate Kwanzaa, provide an Umoja Karamu feast, sponsor Black History Month celebrations, and teach youth rites of passage. They also have parties and provide a step show with an

Africentric motif. There is much more to college life than academics. Greek life is one illustration, but probably the most demanding is in the next chapter on male/female relationships.

CHAPTER SIX

The Power, Passion, and Pain of Black Love

The title of this chapter is also the title of a book that I have written on male/female relationships. It is impossible in one chapter to do justice to something as significant and comprehensive as male/female relationships. I often share with African American students that there is nothing that they will do that will be more challenging in their lives than identifying, developing, nurturing, and maintaining their relationships. I have mentioned to them that graduating, securing employment, developing a career, starting a business, acquiring property, and even raising children will not be as challenging as developing a stable relationship.

In the ideal world, on a college campus, a young man, tall, dark, and handsome, meets a beautiful and sincere African American female and they begin to date. They date all four years of college, and throughout medical and law school. Upon satisfactorily completing professional schools, passing the board and the bar exam, they get married. They have two children who also go off to college and everyone lives happily ever after. This is the ideal world, and it could return to this state if we did it God's way and submitted ourselves to Him. For the Lord loves the family so much that He created the family before he created the church. He hates divorce. God's Word will teach people how to keep their relationship together.

Unfortunately, on many college campuses the ideal is not being enjoyed. A young man meets a young woman and both possess an attitude of "What can you do for me? If you make me feel good then we can stay together. As soon as you stop making me feel good I'm out of here." They play games with each other. They will have sex before marriage and with other people. Someone will get hurt. She may become pregnant. Do they keep the baby? Abortion? Adoption? Frustration will ensue. They will tell their friends that the other person did not make them happy and they will split.

I have conducted over 500 workshops on male/female relationships and have heard about many others. There seems to be the assumption that people can separate Black men from Black women. Some Black women are throwing darts at Black men and believe the major problem in relationships are irresponsible, self-centered, lazy, and destructive Black men.

I wrote *Good Brothers Looking For Good Sisters* because I knew better. I have met many good brothers in my travels around the country. I have heard too many brothers call on talk shows having the same difficulties Black women are having trying to find a good mate. I know that Black men and Black women mirror each other. A Black man could not be a pimp without a prostitute. Nor could a Black man be a loving, God-centered husband without a loving, God-centered wife.

Waiting to Exhale was far more than about irresponsible men. It was also about women who made foolish choices. If Black women nationwide got together and said they were not compromising anymore, that they were raising the level of expectations, and not playing games anymore, people would be amazed at how many boys would become men.

I mentioned in *Restoring the Village, Values, and Commitment: Solutions for the Black Family* that there are four stages in a relationship. They include: selection, romance, problem, and commitment. In this chapter we will only look at one – selection. Many of us do a better job selecting our cars, clothes, houses, careers, and businesses than selecting a mate. In a survey of what Black men and Black women look for in a mate, Black men had the following preference: face, legs, bust, hair and personality. Black women had the following preference: provider, looks, attire, sexual performance, and personality.[1]

What I appreciated most about the above findings is these people were honest. Most people know that the desired answers are personality, values, responsibility, and spirituality. While all of us will say that we value those qualities, unfortunately these were not in our top five. We still live in a very materialistic society where the external is valued more than the internal. When we are honest, we acknowledge that initially we are attracted to each other physically. For many women, even looks were secondary to his ability to provide.

In Larry Davis' book, *Black and Single,* he develops the term "RMV" (Romantic Market Value), and through scientific analysis he points out that individuals' RMV fluctuates. For example, there are two people who look like Michael Jordan, Wesley Snipes, Evander Holyfield and Mike Tyson, but only one is the actual person. Is there any doubt which one has the greatest RMV? One brother who looks like Michael Jordan lives in the rural part of the South and is a laborer. The other person who looks like Michael Jordan earned more than 100 million last year. I wonder if sisters see both brothers with the same RMV? I wonder if both brothers would be able to attract the same type of women? The same is applicable to Mike Tyson, Wesley Snipes and Evander Holyfield.

Unfortunately, on many of our campuses, there are women in particular who not only will have difficult times selecting a mate, but in many cases will graduate from college and not have enjoyed one date. I mentioned previously that if one looks at a kindergarten class one will see an equal number of boys and girls in class. If one looks at the 12th grade graduating class oftentimes there is a 2:1 ratio. That ratio often rises on college campuses.

There are many reasons that brothers play games. First, they play because of the male shortage. Many brothers are cognizant that due to the male shortage some women will compromise their principles. I will never forget meeting a sister who was only 19 years of age. She told me how hard it was to deal with brothers on campus. She said, "I am tired of playing games. I am going home, getting in the bath tub, with my Bible, and have peace with *Him*." I was impressed with her maturity but empathized with her   circumstances.

Many brothers play games because they lack maturity. Some play games because it's a power struggle, and sexism exists within their community. It is very difficult to discuss relationships with a male shortage.

Nothing irritates Black women on college campuses more than the few brothers that do exist who have chosen to date White women. It is even more disheartening to Black women when many of the athletes, some of them with tremendous income-earning potential, also choose to date White women. I have seen parties thrown for athletes, especially professional athletes, where they literally import White women and restrict sisters from entering. It reminds me of a meat market and because many Black women understand that they come from an ancestry of queens, they do not succumb to this level of prostitution.

Unfortunately, some brothers feel that Black women are too hard on them and White women are more complimentary, compromising, understanding, attentive, and fit their definition of beauty: light, long hair, and blue eyes. I have often wondered that since there is a shortage of Black men, if there shouldn't be more African American women dating outside the race? Is it because Black women are more loyal? Is it because White men are more loyal to White women? Do Black men see more beauty in White women than White men see in Black women?

Even within the context of a male shortage on many campuses, there are many good brothers who are overlooked. On a typical campus there are 200 African American students, 120 females and 80 males. The male population includes 40 athletes; 10 brothers who date White women; five who are gay; 15 Greeks; and the remaining 10 are "regular brothers." Ironically, those 10 remaining brothers have the highest GPA and possess the greatest chance to graduate. Yet, on many campuses they are least revered by Black women.

Many brothers say sisters play games too. In my book, *Good Brothers Looking For Good Sisters,* Randolph was my intellectual. He was an engineering student. He was neither an athlete nor a member of a fraternity. He was an average-looking brother and an honor roll student. He loved Black women and would often say that his mother is a Black woman. I have met many Randolphs in my travels to campuses. I have also met others who were irritated and hurt by Black women who have overlooked them for athletes, rappers, and members of fraternities. I have also met some older Randolphs who are no longer engineering students, but are now full-fledged engineers, doctors, lawyers, and computer programmers. They are very cynical toward Black women. They believe Black women only want them now because their "RMV" has improved with salaries in excess of $50,000. Randolph is no longer an engineering student, but a full-fledged engineer who now dates White women.

There are numerous games that are being played between males and females. Some of them are very tragic. I remind high school students that 60 percent of teenage pregnancies occur where there is a five year gap between her age and his. He is between 17 and 25 and she is between 11 and 16. I call those brothers with weak raps because if they had a stronger rap they would rap to a sister their own age. Many girls believe that they are women based upon the size of their bust, butt, and hips. Real women know it's the development of their brain, heart, and spirit.

The games continue from high school to college because people don't learn the lessons. The brothers are a little older between 25 and 30, and the young ladies are now 18 to 21. We now have some career students. They have been in school for almost a decade. They have a car and live off campus. They take an average of six hours per semester and will probably graduate in the next decade. Their favorite prey are young freshman sisters who have had a sheltered environment and have never experienced life away from their parents.

One of the most tragic experiences I have ever observed became a full feature article in *Emerge magazine*. This article was about a freshman student named Kemba who lived a very protective life and attended Hampton University.[2] I have mentioned the popularity enjoyed by many athletes, fraternity brothers, and rappers. There are also older men who are no longer students. Some are drug dealers. They have nice apartments and drive luxury cars. Many young, naive sisters who are trying to impress their female friends and make a statement to their male peers are vulnerable to these male vultures. This becomes a toxic relationship.

While it is true that Randolph as a freshman could not have provided the kind of lifestyle for Kemba, he would have been a more suitable mate. Instead, Kemba chose Peter Hall who not only mesmerized her, but whatever common sense she possessed went out the window. Even the judge could not believe that she was not aware that his lifestyle was due to drug dealing, and that she was involved in drug laundering. The judge sentenced her to 24.5 years in prison while her parents were left with the responsibility of taking care of the child which resulted from this affair. In the previous chapter, I empathized with parents whose children have died while pledging. I also empathize with Kemba's parents and all others who have suffered similar experiences. Parents badger and torture themselves wondering what they did wrong.

It hurts me when I talk to students on campus and hear as well as see that the level of drug selling and consuming along with rampant promiscuity. Some of our students simply lack the maturity of being away from home for the first time, living in dormitories or off-campus where there are few or unenforced rules. I am reminded of my elementary school girlfriend who throughout elementary school and high school had very strict parents. Within two months on a college campus she was addicted to reefer and pregnant.

I used to believe and still say to high school students that they have a lesser chance of becoming pregnant when they have goals and something to lose. I tell students that when they plan on attending Spelman, Howard, Hampton, or any university, that they have a lesser chance of becoming pregnant.

Some of our students are majoring in sex, and minoring in drugs under the auspices of being college students. On some campuses there are more STDs than there are in inner city neighborhoods. Many African American females are now acting like White girls who have a similar pregnancy percentage of ten percent but were aborting the fetus. Historically, African American females kept their babies, but no longer. Cynically speaking, this is another benefit of integration. On many campuses abortion has become synonymous with birth control and parents are often unaware. High school girls may think their babies are going to go away, therefore they do not see a need to tell their mothers, however, college females "know better." African American women are now aborting their babies like their White female peers.

The question we raised in the earlier chapter regarding why some fraternities moved from pledging to hazing is also applicable to why some brothers are running more trains. I am still operating under the premise that these are DuBois' Talented Tenth and the best Black men. I was very concerned when a train took place at one of our best Black colleges. The males took the position it was her fault because she was in the dormitory after hours with suggestive clothing. Brothers, you are in college not the 13th grade; you are a man, not a dog. You can control yourself. There is nothing that can explain why you would be a willing participant in a train being run on a sister. I am appealing to every brother who is reading this book, that if he ever finds himself in this type of situation that he will do everything possible to free his sister of this savagery, even if it requires physical and verbal confrontation from his so-called friends.

I wonder if brothers blame running a train on the White man? If trains are being run by African American college males, heaven forbid what is going on in inner city neighborhoods. In Italian communities there are warnings when people sell drugs the first time, the second time their left wrist is cut. I recommend there would be no warning if you were caught involved in a train. The Fruit of Jesus and the Fruit of Islam would castrate you. I'm sure that that would reduce the problems we're having on many of our campuses. Unfortunately, since my idea is not going to be implemented anytime soon, we appeal to your judgment that after reading this book you will treat women with more respect.

We hope that women will look at the totality of a brother and not just his "RMV." We pray brothers that if a sister asks are you involved with someone else, that you will in the spirit of Maat – tell the truth. Brothers often remind me to tell sisters, three dates don't constitute a relationship and sisters should avoid rushing commitment. We pray that we will see each other the way

God sees us as beautiful, young men and women who have spirit, personality, dreams, aspirations, and goals. Brothers and sisters need to talk and listen to each other. We need to respect and encourage each other. African American men and women need to treat each other the way they want to be treated or how they would want someone to relate to their siblings. Brothers, treat your lady the way you want a brother to treat your sister. Sisters, treat your man the way you want a sister to treat your brother. Friendship should be the first priority of male/female relationships.

Maulana Karenga, the founder of Kwanzaa, reminds us that if we want to find out what the nation is doing all we have to do is look inside of its homes. I would like to extrapolate from that analogy that if you want to find out what the Black nation is doing all you have to do is look at the relationships on campus. If these are our future leaders and this is the way they treat each other, then there is no wonder that our communities look the way they do.

In the next chapter we will look at nation building. What good is it to have a degree and no commitment to the liberation of African people?

CHAPTER SEVEN

DuBois' Talented Tenth

There are 1,000 African American students who attend this university. It is late September. It has been a month since the students arrived back on campus. There have been many parties and four football games since school began. Now it is time to elect officers for the Black Student Union and plan the agenda for this upcoming year.

This is the first meeting of the Black Student Union. This university has a great tradition of advocacy. Thirty years ago African American college students barricaded themselves in the administration office and demanded that their concerns be heard. They wanted a Black Student Union because they felt that the larger student government was not representing their needs. They wanted an African American studies department that would be accredited, offer a major, and choose the director. They wanted their Black Student Union to be housed in their own Black house. They demanded 15 percent of their regular student government budget which reflected their percentage on campus. They wanted Martin Luther King Jr.'s birthday to be honored on campus by having no classes. They wanted a mandatory course for all students on multiculturalism taught by a multicultural faculty. They demanded greater financial aid to African American students and the development of an academic support center with free tutoring. They also demanded that 15 percent of the airtime on the university radio station be allocated for African American programming.

The history of liberation movements were primarily led by youth and the poor. When people become older and earn more income, they tend to become conservative, middle class, and have a greater desire to maintain their standard of living. Minister Louis Farrakhan has often mentioned what do youth and poor people care about the odds.

A review of the liberation movements in America, in the '50s and '60s shows the marchers, sit-ins, the lunch counters, and public demonstrators, to be primarily young people, predominately students. Jesse Jackson Sr. and Stokely Carmichael (Kwame Toure) were students who became active with SCLC (Southern Christian Leadership Conference) and SNCC (Student Nonviolent Coordinating Committee) respectively. Along with CORE (Congress of Racial Equality) and the NAACP (National Association of the Advancement of Colored People). If you look at our liberation struggle in Azania, South Africa, it was students who did not want to speak the oppressor's language of Afrikaan. It was students who protested about the poor resources that were allocated to their school.

Young people filled with hope, zeal, possibility, and a thirst for education have always been the catalyst for our liberation movement. Each "Joshua" generation will have its day to make an impact on society, but it is a fleeting moment and once it passes it may never be retrieved.

The Black Student Union meeting is about to begin, with the purpose of electing the president, two vice-presidents, a secretary, and a treasurer. Unfortunately, only 14 people attend the meeting. Pertaining to the Greek chapter, I have wondered how the founders felt as they watched their fraternity or sorority hazing someone to death. I now wonder how the founding (BSU) students would feel observing the apathy of new African American students toward being involved in their Student Union.

One of the frequent questions Black Student Union presidents ask me on my visit to their campus is "how can they increase student involvement?" Why do almost 1,000 people (including neighboring campuses and the local community) attend a party? Yet the Black Student Union can barely secure a quorum to vote for officers and only a handful attend a lecture? The questions come from young people, some less than 20 years of age. Yet they sound like tired, worn-out, and burned-out veterans.

I often wonder how young people become burned-out before their 21st birthday. I have seen students burn out because of their compassion, zeal, and love for our people. Their frustration is a result of our people possessing misplaced priorities. I have witnessed Black Student Union presidents call my office; negotiate the fee; sign the contract; develop the fliers; distribute the fliers; convince people to come; secure the building; provide the equipment; make arrangements for a reception; provide round-trip transportation for me from the airport; and after all the activities have concluded, return home and study for tomorrow's test.

Over the past two decades I have often wondered where are those student leaders. Did they graduate from college? Are they actively involved in the liberation struggle? Did they become apathetic and cynical? Have they sold out to corporate America, individualism, and materialism? Are they so frustrated with our people that they will never join another African American organization?

The meeting begins. The current president who is burned-out and will not be running for a second term, asks if there are any people present who want to run for one of the four positions? Six hands are raised. After 30 minutes of deliberation four students are elected to office to represent an African American student body of 1,000.

DuBois' Talented Tenth

With the new officers in place, the Black Student Union plan the agenda for the upcoming year. They suggest having a membership drive in October, a Kwanzaa feast in December, a workshop on Dr. King in January, two speakers in February along with a play, a week's series of Black movies and a rap concert. In March they want a speaker for Women's Month. They also are considering writing articles regularly for the school newspaper. These articles will be written from a Black perspective. They will teach Black history and culture on Saturdays to African American children who live in this college town.

There is a great degree of discussion that this agenda is too demanding for 14 students and that more effort should be placed on a membership drive. This leads into a discussion of student apathy that dominates the rest of the evening.

Almost every Black Student Union president has tried to convince me that there is no student body more apathetic than theirs. My experience has shown me that apathy transcends region, and that we are just as apathetic in the South, North, East, or West.

Although some BSU organizations are suffering because of low membership, there is still some good news to report. I have observed many student unions where they are doing excellent work regardless of the number of students involved. Over the years, I have tried to give numerous suggestions and words of encouragement to Black student leaders. If 1,000 students had attended the Black Student Union meeting then African Americans would not have their current problems. If Black people were more concerned about their liberation than partying, our problems would be solved. If Black people were more loyal to the Black Student Union than to their fraternity or sorority then we would not be experiencing the present challenges. I have to remind student leaders that the reason that we have the Black Student Union is not only because of White supremacy, but because of its repercussions to our people.

One of the consequences of White supremacy has been apathy. We are no longer convinced that we can make a difference. What would be more detrimental is if the few African Americans who survived this mental slavery also conceded. Suppose no one had attended the BSU meeting. The 14 students have to believe that they can make a difference and provide quality programming for the other 986. I remind them that they are either part of the problem or the solution. Life is still very simple. If we give up we automatically lose; only if we dare to struggle do we have any chance of winning. I give the students the scenario that it's the bottom of the 9th inning, there are two outs, and that there is an 0 and 2 count on the batter. They have their best pitcher pitching and we have our worst batter at the plate. We have to believe we are going to start a rally and win the game. We need to garner the same faith as Nelson Mandela and Geronimo Pratt (Ji Jaga) who endured 27 years of incarceration while innocent.

I feel good when I say this and initially they respond as if they understand. But I wonder how they feel days, weeks, and months later. I have been in their shoes. I was the Black Student Union president of the university I attended and apathy was thick as gravy. But I used my collegiate experience like a minor league training experience preparing me for a big league revolution. If I thought it was challenging trying to organize DuBois' Talented Tenth, it would be even more challenging trying to organize the masses of our people, some who are living in projects, others who will kill you for another fix, and some like Clarence Thomas who believe they have theirs and you have yours to get.

When students contract with my office for me to speak, my office sends them a list of promotional strategies to make the event more successful. While Christianity has taught me that if only two believers are in the room then He will make it successful, I'm still motivated to speak, but I'm also very much aware that there is very little I can do about the numbers once I arrive. We suggest to students that they appeal to African American faculty members to either require their classes to be in attendance or to provide extra credit. We also suggest inviting the fraternity and sorority leaders to participate in the program. There is a good chance their members will also attend. In addition, we recommend inviting the gospel choir for an opening and closing selection. If the closing selection is not included then the choir may leave before the speaker.

Black people love food. Notice, I did not say refreshments. I have witnessed excellent attendance when food that African Americans enjoy has been provided. Unfortunately, I have also noticed students who did not attend the lecture, mysteriously arrive for the food. Safeguards need to be implemented to avoid this abuse.

One college went as far as to have a party after I spoke, but only for students who attended the lecture. That reminded me of what we used to do with LeRoi Jones (Imamu Baraka) and the Congress of African People (CAP) in the early 70s. We would sponsor parties for the community and every hour on the hour we would turn on the lights and give a five minute political analysis of what's affecting our people. Then we would turn the lights off again and party for another 55 minutes. We would repeat that throughout the night. Sometimes we have to meet people where they are. Jesus met the Samaritan woman where she was (at the well) because she may never have entered the temple.

DuBois' Talented Tenth

Selection of the topic is critical. Many times the president and committee of the BSU are very conscious and want a topic that reflects their level of consciousness, but it may not reflect the mindset of the 986 people they represent. The majority may prefer a discussion of male/female relationships, economics, hip-hop, or retention strategies. However, the committee may want to discuss African history, philosophy, languages, or racism. As an experienced speaker I peruse the audience and realize I must weave all these interests and make them palatable for everyone.

The selection of the time and day for a program are also critical. While there is no ideal time, day, or temperature for apathetic students, my 25 years of experience has taught me that midweek at noon is better for commuter colleges and midweek at 7p.m. is better for colleges with dormitories. It has been very frustrating to me to speak on the same day as a football or basketball game or right before finals when many students are cramming. There have even been some engagements where I was brought in on a particular night which was a popular Black TV night. How unfortunate that the liberation struggle has to consider such factors. Harriet Tubman, Marcus Garvey and others did not have to consider such issues.

When I was at ISU, I read the work of Amilcar Cabral, Frantz Fanon, Paulo Freire, Elijah Muhammad, Marcus Garvey, and others. I surmised from their writings that leaders should not organize the masses of people with ideas, but by providing basic goods and services. Mostly intellectuals argue for hours about capitalism, communism, socialism, racism, sexism, classism, colorism, Christianity, Islam, Buddhism, and Hinduism. The masses of people are concerned about food, clothing, shelter, employment, and recreation.

At ISU, the university did not provide an evening meal on Sunday. Our group Unity, met that need and provided dinner for African American students on campus. Coincidentally, when they came to receive their dinner, they also received a lecture series and a full book display that we provided. They came to eat food, and we used it as bait to nourish their mind.

We have to find ways to market Blackness like companies market soap, toothpaste, or any product. Most people join organizations because they feel that they are going to accrue benefits. If fraternity and sorority members are honest, they will admit that they didn't join them because they wanted to give back to the community. They joined because they saw concrete benefits that they were going to receive. The question then becomes: What benefit would anybody receive by being a member of the Black Student Union? If I become a member of Alpha Phi Alpha,

I have the brotherhood of more than 150,000 other brothers. I also may have special inroads with the Alpha Angels and the sisters of AKA. My fraternity will be giving a party at least twice a month which provides me free admission and I get a chance to step, not only at our parties, but at others sponsored by other fraternities and sororities. I will be one of a chosen few who will wear T-shirts, sweaters, and other paraphernalia only eligible for Alphas. Depending upon how well I step, I may be as popular as an athlete.

African American student leaders have to think like this, and ask themselves how they can compete against that mindset? What can we provide for that type of student who has a *what's in it for me* mentality? People who are committed possess a different value system. They are less concerned about themselves and more concerned about the deplorable conditions of their people. I must mention though, that some African American leaders, both students and professionals, have a "lightning bug" personality. While initially, they were attracted to the movement for sincere reasons, they now enjoy the fame, prestige, their position affords them. We must be careful not to criticize students who seek accolades during the step show and deny we are not seeking the same glory at the Black Power Conference, when we are acknowledged for our great efforts.

The mistake of many sincere African American leaders is assuming the masses have their values. Therefore, the leaders continue to design programs that they think are for the good of the collective while ignoring the research of Cabral, Fanon, Friere, Muhammad, Garvey and others. These leaders realized that they must address their personal desires. We make the same mistake in misdiagnosing the majority of White people. We continue to treat them from our "can we all just get along" value system, when it is obvious that they are obsessed with power and control.

In the Greek chapter, we mentioned people also value things they earn. Not only does it appear that there are fewer benefits being a member of the Black Student Union than other social organizations, but there are no requirements for membership. Students historically had to pledge to become a member of a Greek organization before the in take process. I wondered why someone would say, "I will be a Que to the day I die" and would welcome being branded. It appears that people are more committed to being members of Greek fraternities or sororities than members of the BSU or to the Lord. Could one reason be because there are few if any requirements? Anyone can be a member by simply attending the meeting. At some colleges, students are members whether or not they ever attend a meeting! People put a cross around their neck and say they believe in Jesus. You can tell from their "fruit," not their talk and symbols, that it's a facade. Going to church does not make you a Christian, just as attending a BSU meeting does not make one committed to the liberation struggle.

If members continue to base their allegiance on what they can *get* from the organization and not what they can *give* back to it, we will continue to have institutions where 10 percent of the people are doing 90 percent of the work. What concerns me is when the 10 percent becomes so comfortable with that scenario that they begin to personify the "woe is me" mentality. It appears that some leaders have no desire to change the equation because they like to be in the position of a martyr and indispensable. We must learn how to delegate and develop new leaders. I have seen excellent BSUs fold because new leadership was not mentored.

I have never liked the word *struggle*. It is not the end, we struggle to achieve *freedom*. Freedom is not riding White-owned buses in Montgomery, going to White-controlled schools in Topeka, Kansas, and closing the Negro Baseball League so that a few primadonnas can buy twenty-bedroom houses. Freedom entails self-definition. We must define success, beauty, and our icons. Freedom means building institutions that are self-sufficient. Freedom affords the opportunity to develop one's talents to their full capacity.

Our problem is that most of our people cannot define freedom. If we had 100 people in an audience and asked each of them to give their definition of freedom, we would have 100 different definitions. That is why we have not achieved it.

One of the reasons that African Americans remain so confused is that schools teach more than academics; they teach Eurocentric values. Non-African schools are designed to either destroy African people or make them committed to White values. I know you don't like those options but that is why schools are designed. Let me describe the Design/Purpose Machine.

<u>Destroy</u>

* African American children enter kindergarten eager to learn, but quickly are discouraged, labeled hyperactive, and tracked.

* African American children's scores decline after third grade.

* A disproportionate number of African American children are placed in special education.

* A disproportionate percentage of African American youth are suspended.

* A disproportionate number of African American youth drop out or are pushed out of high school.

* A disproportionate number of African American youth graduate illiterate.

DuBois' Talented Tenth

White Values

* An Eurocentric definition of beauty that includes light skin, blue eyes, and long, straight hair.

* A belief that Greece is the origin of civilization.

* A belief that White colleges are better than Black colleges.

* A belief that White businesses are better than Black businesses.

* A belief that Jesus looks life Michael Angelo's cousin.

* A belief that African Americans can't build a nice stable neighborhood, therefore, they must live with Whites.

* A belief that working for White corporate America downtown or in the suburbs is better than working for an African American organization in the inner city.

* African American politicians are more concerned with not offending Whites than serving their larger loyal African American constituency.

The last thing I want to do in this chapter is to leave the readers with something so depressing as a Design/ Purpose Machine. So the question becomes, "How do we defeat this machine?" The only way to solve any problem is through awareness. Once we are aware of the purpose of schools we have a much better chance of defending ourselves. If we look at Africans from the continent, one of the ways they attempt to defeat the Design/Purpose Machine is to shy away from courses in the liberal arts, which are more subjective and lies about Columbus discovering America and Abraham Lincoln freeing the slaves. They primarily major in the natural sciences and business which is more objective. To give you a sense of self, begin to immerse yourselves in your history and culture to learn as much as you possibly can about the greatness of your own people. The good news is that a people who know their history and culture have a much greater chance of resisting racism and White supremacy.

Begin to develop a mentality of acquisition. Your objective is to acquire as much information as you possibly can from schools, with the sole objective of returning home to your community or country to make it a better place. What good is it for African Americans to have the greatest number of Africans in the world with degrees, but who have very little commitment to the race? As much as I respect DuBois, I'm glad Marcus Garvey challenged DuBois and allowed the masses of people to benefit from both schools of thought: nationalism and integration. Marcus Garvey was a strong advocate of building cultural institutions and economic empowerment.

DuBois' Talented Tenth

I am very concerned about DuBois' Talented Tenth who may not live, work, spend, volunteer, and invest in the Black community. Some of DuBois' Talented Tenth seem unable to relate to their less fortunate brothers and sisters who were unable to attend college. Has "miseducation" separated those to whom much has been given from the least of these? Our struggle for freedom has to be waged against racism, sexism, and classism. How can brothers fight for justice against White supremacy and oppress their women? How can middle class Black leaders fight for justice, but cut deals that only benefit them? During their eras Garvey and Malcolm were critical of "House Negroes" who don't represent "Field Negroes." Today, Farrakhan is still critical of this same group. How can African American teachers be against school vouchers, but send their child to a private school? How can African American leaders build a freedom movement and ask the oppressor for a grant to finance it?

Because of the Design/Purpose Machine, people like Ward Connerly and Clarence Thomas have attended K-12 grade and college, and have never been required to give back to the African American community. If I had it my way no African American could graduate from college without reading the book of Nehemiah. No African American student could graduate from college without a plan or blueprint on how they are going to empower the community. No African American student could graduate from college if they could not parallel what they have learned in their major, and how it can be applied to a problem that exists within the African American community. Schools have taught rugged individualism. Remember the brothers and sisters who were pledging? *None* of them were able to cross over until *all* of them were able to cross over. If one knew the information but their brothers and sisters did not in many cases, you were the one who was beaten. The lesson that fraternities and sororities were teaching is Biblical (my brother's keeper) and Africentric (Ujima - collective work and responsibility).

In closing, I am very worried about this generation of African American college students. There is a rumor that this could be the first generation that may never exceed their parents in academic achievement. It is the first generation of African American youth who may never leave home. When I was in college I would have been embarrassed to return home from college without a degree. I had too much pride. But there are some African American college students who have no problems dropping out of college for a myriad of reasons: the teacher did not like me; I didn't like the food; I needed to come home and find myself; I'd rather live at home; there was nothing to do socially. They don't seem embarrassed about coming home.

This could be the first generation of African American youth who are soft on resisting racism. Unfortunately, many of our parents wanted to make it better for their children, therefore they gave them more things and less time. They forgot to teach them their history. African American college students need to remember Harriet Tubman and her 19 trips from the South to the North. They need to remember that Nat Turner wanted to be free so much that even when everyone else was caught, he buried himself in the ground for six extra weeks before he was finally caught. The Jews have a motto called "Never Forget." They believe that if they forget the six million Jews who died in Germany that they will lose Israel. We have a similar motto. We just dropped the word *never* and want to *forget* almost a hundred million Africans who died in the slave trade. We call our holocaust Maafa. We are the offspring of the ancestors who would not die. We are their answered prayers. The major challenge for the 21st century is how we will repay them for their sacrifice.

If I had it my way, no African American college student could graduate from college until he/she went to Ghana or Senegal and went through The Door of No Return. Students would be required to lie down on the floor of the dungeons and try to listen to the floor, which would tell them what our people endured. The floor would tell them about how much blood was shed. My desire is that African American college students have an opportunity to lay on the floor and make promises to their ancestors, who endured four months in this dungeon, three months on the slave ship, and 246 years of slavery. These students would promise that they would no longer complain about the food, professors, their social life, parents or whatever else they had been complaining about. They would graduate from college with honors. From this day forward, they would be committed to the liberation of African people. Many White students visit Europe for the summer. I am very much aware that many African American students can't afford to visit Africa, but there are some who can. There are also internships and special programs that are free. Most African Americans even when they graduate and earn a good income will choose some exotic Caribbean island over Africa. For many of our people we lost our minds – our memory when we went through "the door of no return." Some African Americans say, "I'm not African, my family came from Mississippi." Until people of African descent make it back "home," Whoopi Goldberg and Ward Connerly, please watch "*Sankofa*" and "*Daughter of the Dust.*" Malcolm X taught African Americans decades ago that *where* you are born, does not determine *who* you are!

Congratulations! If you have read this far in the book, I pray you have mastered retention strategies and are committed to the liberation of African people. The next chapter explores the numerous options that await you after graduation.

CHAPTER EIGHT

Life After College

African Americans are 17 percent of the K-12 grade students, but only 10 percent of college students, and unfortunately only six percent of graduate students. In addition, only four percent of the doctoral students are African American. I have observed many types of students on college campuses. There are some students who are very clear about what they want to do after college. They have selected majors that have given them a sense of direction. Students who have a desire to become doctors and attorneys are very clear that after college they are going to medical and law school. They knew as freshmen there would be four years of graduate school.

There are other students who are not quite clear about their major. Therefore, they are not clear on what they will do after graduation. There is also the group in the middle that are fairly confident of their selection for their major but are not quite clear on their plans after graduation. Many students are in a quandary between graduate school and employment.

In order to have a successful transition after college there are certain resources that college students should consider. I would first recommend that every African

American college student subscribe to *Black Collegian* magazine. It not only provides contemporary articles on Black college life, but also provides tremendous resources for employment and graduate school positions. The magazine provides an annual survey of the top 100 employers for African Americans. It ranks the demand of various majors. A job finder database is available along with a listing of internships. A thorough analysis of graduate school admission requirements and financial assistance is also provided.

I am not discouraging college students reading *Vibe, Source, Rap Pages,* or any other magazine, but I am disappointed that many of our students are reading those magazines and not reading *Black Collegian* and *Black Issues in Higher Education.*

My second recommendation is for college students to visit the college placement office or college career center. Unfortunately, two places many African American students don't take advantage of are the tutorial center and the college placement office. There are far more people in the Union socializing than the above. I believe that there are numerous benefits visiting the placement office early in your college career. First, it confirms you believe you will graduate.

The scripture in Romans 4:17 reminds us, "We need to call that that does not exist as if it were." College students need to claim the fact they are going to graduate.

Life After College

They need to claim that reality very early in their collegiate experience. It is a confident and bold step for a college freshman or sophomore to visit the college career or placement office because they want to take advantage of all the resources that exist because they will be graduating from college.

Many colleges have career centers because many students are unsure of their major and their related careers. There is also the opportunity to take an inventory test to measure your interest and to gain a better understanding of your strengths and weaknesses. It disappoints me to talk to so many graduating seniors who are still not quite sure if they chose the right major. I have talked to so many students who have decided that since they had taken so many courses in a particular field, that they might as well continue to complete the degree in that field. That rationale does not make sense to me. If a student knows that he/she is going in the wrong direction, why does he/she continue driving in that path? I would think that as soon as he/she found that he/she was going in the wrong direction he/she would make a change.

Dennis Kimbro says, "A job is what you do with your days, but a career is what you do with your life." I am very disappointed with large numbers of college graduates who are working jobs that they do not like just for money. It is imperative to access your interests and find a career that you love so much that you would be willing to do it for free, but because you do it so well you are paid.

My third recommendation is that in the freshman year students should identify professors and faculty who can become mentors. They can help students with career decisions and write letters of recommendation. It is so disappointing to me that many African American college students have not learned to network and to create alliances and relationships. George Fraser has written the excellent book Success Runs in Our Race which gives strategies on networking and its significance.

My fourth recommendation is that during the sophomore year, the student should visit the placement office and identify companies with internships that complement their major. Students need to balance theory from their major with practical experience. While income has to be considered, sometimes it may be better to choose a company that does not pay interns, but will provide an excellent experience and possible future employment. How unfortunate that so many African American college students during the summer are working at fast food chains and other unrelated activities to their major versus doing the necessary homework and identifying companies that provide internships that parallel their major and their careers.

I believe the junior year is critical to the success of the senior year, just as the 9th frame in bowling is to the

10th frame. There are too many juniors who are wasting this year and not looking at the larger picture, the global economy, and the marketplace. I have seen too many students wait until their senior year and some actually graduate from college before they visit the college placement office or consider graduate school.

During this very important junior year, I would strongly recommend that students secure two lists of companies. One list is about those that hire a large number of people in their major. The other list is about those that hire a large number of African Americans. Students should send them letters of interest.

I am also critical of universities because on many campuses the college placement office and career center are the best kept secrets in town. They have a wealth of information, but is poorly promoted and circulated. I commend those universities that in their freshman orientation not only do they mention their college placement office, but also include it on the tour. They don't leave to chance that students will ultimately find this institution. I think that if more freshmen were given information about the college placement office, they would not wait until they are graduating before they make their first visit.

My fifth recommendation is that during the junior year the student should secure a copy of the Peterson Guides. These guides will give a wealth of information about graduate school, admission requirements, assistant-ships, and other pertinent information. Students should secure workbooks, test taking guides, and computer soft-ware on the graduate record exam (GRE). Whites score almost 400 greater than African American students, due in my opinion to a lack of preparation. Unfortunately, many African American students don't decide that they want to attend graduate school until very late in the second semester of their senior year. I mentioned earlier that the junior year is the foundational year, and that is the time to seriously consider graduate school. Students have a much better chance of securing an assistantship if the decision is made in their junior year. Financial aid is very scarce at the graduate level. It is also very important that the student's GRE scores are sent to the school very early in the first semester of his/her senior year.

Students who need the most money, ironically, are the students who apply later. As we are now in the Second Reconstruction with the rollback of affirmative action and other "safety net" programs many universities are no longer offering racial scholarships and admission preferences.

The other two major requirements for successful admission into graduate school are letters of recommendation and writing a letter of purpose. Successful mentoring will greatly benefit students securing positive letters of recommendation. The letter of purpose requires clarity of thought. The student needs to be able to articulate what it is that he/she would like to study in graduate school. Literally this is a written interview where the students describes his/her collegiate experience and how it has given him/her a thirst for additional knowledge in a particular area that he/she would like to pursue. As the student carefully reads the Peterson Guides and discusses with them faculty members, he/she can secure copies of former students' Statements of Purpose that will help him/her in designing their own.

I have talked to many parents who have told me that their child wants to go to graduate school because he/she does not want to work and wants to remain a student indefinitely. Some students are not ready for the pressures of the real world and have grown comfortable with the fact that their parents will simply write them a check to pursue their education. I have even met students who wanted to be college professors, which in most cases will require a Ph.D., for the sole reason that they will only have to teach three or four classes a semester and work a maximum of 12 to 20 hours per week.

I believe that a student who visited the college career center as a freshman, secured an internship as a sophomore, and corresponded with companies and/or reviewed the Peterson Guides in preparation for graduate school during his/her junior year is in a very good position as they move into their senior year. I have talked to thousands of seniors and some of them have no idea what they will be doing after college. They have no idea where they're going to work and for whom.

On the other hand, I have met students who have completed an excellent internship in their junior year, and the employer was so pleased with their work performance that they offered them positions. It is a good experience to be a graduating senior and during the first semester already know your employer, where you will work, what type of work, and your salary. Why should athletes be the only employees sought after during the draft?

I have always felt that there was too wide a gap between the classroom and the workplace. While I'm more understanding of this gap in elementary school, I believe that cooperative education at the high school level and internships at the collegiate level are imperative in order to close this gap and make education more practical. There are too many graduating seniors who have not spent any hours during college in the workplace utilizing the theory that they have acquired for the past four years. Graduating seniors who have decided that they do not want to attend graduate school and have not taken advantage of internships should register themselves with as many job placement services as possible. They should also place their resumé on-line.

Those students who receive a larger number of job offers have been successful for several reasons. First, they have secured an excellent GPA. Second, they understand that the workplace is similar to a meat market, and they recognize what their employers are looking for in a perspective employee. Following are some of the major attributes that employers are seeking: an excellent grade point average, computer literacy, good writing and oral communication skills, leadership qualities, organizational skills, analytical thinking and problem solving, affluence in a foreign language, a team player, energetic, and someone who appreciates diversity.

One of the components of making a successful transition from college to the world of work is how successfully one handles the interview. There is an excellent manual titled, *The Fifty Most Commonly Asked Questions For The Employment Interview.* Many students are inadequately prepared for what could be the most important meeting of their career – The All Important Interview. The college placement office not only has many resource materials on interviewing skills, but it also has video tapes to show positive successful interviews and mistakes that need to be avoided.

Just as we have discussed earlier that America is a test-taking country, and that we may be the only race that views the test for the very first time on test day, we may also be the only race that is involved in an interview without any practice or preparation. Many effective college placement officers even provide role playing experiences where students can practice before the actual interview. The most important component of a successful interview is for the student to be cognizant of the skills that he/she can bring to that company. Note: the student should not just be cognizant of his/her skills, but knowledgeable about the skills that he/she possesses that would benefit that company.

When a prospective employer asks, "What can you offer our corporation?" The student's answer should not be general. Before the interview, the student should have a working knowledge of that company's product line, history, operating procedures, strengths, and weaknesses. Then he/she should be able to dissect and apply his/her particular skills that would complement the company. It is my personal desire that every African American work for the race and not be part of this meat market experience. However, I am very much aware that presently, African American businesses cannot employ all of our youth, especially since we only spend three percent of our $460 billion dollars with Black businesses. I am also very much aware that the desired opening salary for many college students exceeds what many African American employers can provide.

It is my sincere hope that African American businesses can continue to grow so that we can be more competitive against the Fortune 500 companies for DuBois' Talented Tenth. It is also my desire that African American college students will be more committed to the race than they are to the dollar and will consider taking a smaller offer for the long term benefit of their people. It concerns me that many African American students tell me they can't afford to teach our children, but expect White females to educate them.

The economy of the 21st century will be much different from what we have ever experienced. This new information age and global economy will be more competitive and volatile. In 1920, a person could literally work the same job for 40 years without being retrained and receive a pension. In 1960, a person may have been retrained three times before receiving a pension. In this current economy, job descriptions are changing every five years and a person may have to be retrained seven to ten times over a 40 year career and will not receive a pension. Before 1964, African American college students were primarily restricted to education, ministering, medicine, and law. Two of the major fields that were excluded from them were the fields of business and engineering. In this present economy, the majors that have the greatest demand are accounting, all forms of engineering, business management, and marketing.

Before the Civil Rights Act of 1964, our parents and grandparents did not even dream of an internship with corporate America in their sophomore year and a job offering more than $30,000 a year upon graduation. These are now available to this current generation of African American students. At the same time, many of our parents were able to secure employment with one company and they remained there until they retired. This current generation will not enjoy that stability nor a pension. The economy is much too volatile and competitive. These are the best of times and the worst of times depending upon the student's preparation, discipline, habits, and faith.

Congratulations! You have finally made it. It is your graduation day. Four to six years ago a large number of freshmen entered college with you. As you look around almost 70 percent of them are not present. You have achieved your goal, but it has not been easy. As you listen to the graduation speaker you are thinking about your freshman year when you almost didn't make it. There were several times when you wanted to quit, but your belief in yourself, your parents, and the Lord pulled you through. You know that you're not graduating because you're smarter than all those not present. You remember the times when you left the cafeteria table or the union where you were playing cards. You remember when you got up early Saturday morning after partying Friday night. You put in the hours and that's why you are here on this glorious Saturday afternoon.

Life After College

It has been a major challenge financially. Every year the funding became smaller while the cost of an education continued to increase, but you had made too much of an investment of time and money to turn back and so you endured. You now have student loans that exceed $15,000 and yet you don't even have a full time job. You look out at the audience and you see your parents, aunts, uncles, and siblings. Only one of them has a college degree. Your two siblings are also in college.

Today is a very special day, but you don't have much time to enjoy it because there are decisions that must be made. Do you go out into the marketplace? Lord knows you need the money and the first payment of the loan becomes due in six months. You wonder how long it will take to find a job? Your friends said they had to wait almost three months before they got a job close to their major. Even then they were only paid $21,000 a year. You knew you should have continued your dream toward the NBA so that you could be signing a $50 million contract. Five years of college and you're only making $21,000? You have friends who didn't go to college or only stayed a year and they are making $20,000. Did you make a mistake?

You look over at Randolph who's graduating from the engineering department. His salary will be $34,000. Your girlfriend Renee who's graduating from the accounting department, will be making $28,000. Renee was smart enough during her last two years of college to secure an internship with a Big Eight accounting firm. While the income was not as good as she would have liked, during the summer it allowed her to observe the company and vice versa. Two years later they decided it was mutually beneficial for Renee to continue to work for them, but this time no longer as an intern but as a staff accountant. She promised she would pursue her CPA. They promised her a $10,000 increase upon completion. Renee has aspirations of opening up her own accounting firm and becoming an entrepreneur.

You majored in criminal justice. You could go out and secure employment in your field at the local jail, but you also have graduate school desires with the hopes of becoming a college professor or going to law school and becoming an attorney. You may have to sit out a year because you waited too late to secure an assistantship. You also feel it may be wise to stay out a year not only to pay off some of your bills, but because you are tired of school and need a break. You have been in the classroom since pre-school and now you're 23 years of age. It has been a long 20 years of ditto sheets, text books, true/false, and multiple choice questions.

You keep thinking about that speaker who came to your campus during Black History Month who kept raising the question, "Why is it that our best Black minds work for White people?" Why don't our best Black minds work for the race? You can't seem to shake that question, but you wonder who in the Black community can hire you with a BA in criminal justice and could pay $21,000 a year?

That speech won't let you go and you are reminded when he said our community needs more Black teachers, entrepreneurs, doctors, and computer programmers. But you don't want to be a teacher. The children are too bad, teachers are not respected, and they are underpaid. Let someone else teach them. Your mind begins to wonder if there is some relationship between the miseducation of our children and them ending up in the criminal justice system. You then ask yourself "Do I want to prevent the problem or maintain it and receive a payroll check?"

The speaker also told you to be careful thinking and not confuse needs with wants. People like Renee wants to quit and start their own businesses, but may be unable to do so if she becomes deep in debt to Visa, a car note, and a mortgage. Your mind wonders, how could you live off $10.00 a week in college, but now in corporate America, can't live off $30,000 a year?

The president of the alumni chapter is now speaking and appealing for you not to forget the institution that helped to make a difference in your life. All you can think of is the $15,000 that you owe, and he wants you to make a contribution. You know you should. The college believed in you and admitted you with low test scores and a poor GPA. They believed you had potential and this day proves they are correct. But how can you contribute with a $15,000 debt and no job?

It's getting closer to the time for you to walk across the stage and receive your degree. You look around the sea of students and all your friends you were able to meet. You wonder if you will be able to maintain their friendships. Where will everyone be in ten years? Will we forget each other? Will we move too far geographically to meet again?

As they begin to near your name, you have just decided that you do want to take the GRE. You think maybe some university will like my score, have mercy on me and give me the money for the fall. You feel you're not ready to work everyday. You would rather stay in school a little longer and maybe become a professor. You then ask yourself "Why is it that I don't want to teach nine-year-old boys, but I would not mind teaching college students?" Is it the money? Prestige? Is it the age of the students? Is it easier? A part of you says it's all of that and a bag of chips.

You really would like to marry Renee, but you're not sure you're ready. She seems to be very clear on her career and priorities. She has her life all planned and oftentimes wants to plan your life. You can't go out like that. A man has to be a man, whatever that means.

They suddenly call out your name and there is a thunderous ovation from your family who were not supposed to clap until the very end. It startles you and you begin to walk across the stage to receive your degree. It seems as if it's taking you forever to walk across the stage, but it also seems it took forever for you to reach this moment in your life. Each step you take, you think about your plans after college. Will I get married? Will I work for the state? Do I go to grad school?

You can't shake that speaker. You keep saying, "If our best Black minds don't live, work, spend, volunteer, and invest, how can our communities be anything else but ghettos?" It's unfortunate but you're 23 years of age with a college degree and still uncertain about your career. You spent so much time trying to graduate and partying that you didn't make it to the placement office. Your parents seem very clear. They told you that you could stay in their house until your 18th birthday, but on your 18th birthday you had to leave, hopefully to go to college. While they allowed you to come back for every vacation and said it's not a problem for you to return home after graduation, it's sort of understood that you are only supposed to stay until you start working and get yourself together.

You don't know if you have it together yet. Maybe you and one of your frat brothers can live together because you know you're not ready to get married. You don't care what Renee says. You don't want to get married until you are settled in your career.

What you would like to do is to talk to that speaker again. There are some questions that you did not get a chance to ask him when he came to your campus. How does a Black male become a "man" in White America? How does he avoid compromising his values and his principles? You know he's probably not available, but he said God was never busy. You have not talked to God in a long time and don't know if He's available. What do you say to someone you haven't talked to in the past six years?

The president of the university puts the degree in your hand and says, "Well done." A voice in the background says, "Well done good and faithful servant." You still don't know what you are going to do with your life after college but you do know Who does. The first thing that you plan to do after the dinner and after the hoopla has died down is get on your knees and thank Him for these collegiate years and to ask Him "What do *You* want me to do with my life?"

REFERENCES

CHAPTER TWO

1) *The African American Education Data Book, Volume I,* Frederick Patterson Research Institute of UNCF, Fairfax, Virginia, 1997, p. 234.

2) ibid., p. 62.

3) ibid., p. 73.

4) ibid., p. 393.

5) ibid., p. 115.

CHAPTER THREE

1) Charles Cherry, *Excellence Without Excuse,* Fort Lauderdale: International Scholastic Press, 1993, p. 56.

2) op. cit., *The African American Education Data Book,* p. 231.

CHAPTER FOUR

1) Clinita Ford. ed. *Student Retention.* Tallahassee: CNJ Associates, 1996, pp. 2, 28, 221, 302.

2) Jawanza Kunjufu, *Countering the Conspiracy to Destroy Black Boys, Volume IV*, Chicago: African American Images, 1994, p. 35.

3) *Black Issues in Higher Education*, July 14, 1994, p. 62.

4) op. cit., *The African American Educational Data Book,* pp. 10, 27-33, 63, 123.

5) *Jawanza Kunjufu, Critical Issues in Educating African American Youth,* Chicago: African American Images, 1989, p. 12.

6) op. cit., Clinita Ford, pp. 12, 16, 218, 298-303.

CHAPTER FIVE

1) Web site of the National Pan-Hellenic Council.

2) *Black Issues in Higher Education,* June 12, 1997, p. 20.

3) ibid., pp. 18-19.

4) ibid., pp. 21-22.

CHAPTER SIX

1) Jawanza Kunjufu, *The Power, Passion, and Pain of Black Love,* Chicago: African American Images, 1993, pp. 91-92.

2) Jawanza Kunjufu, *Restoring the Village, Values, and Commitment: Solutions for the Black Family,* Chicago: African American Images, 1996, p. 92.

3) *Emerge Magazine,* May, 1996, pp. 24-53.

NOTES

NOTES

NOTES

NOTES

NOTES

NOTES

NOTES

NOTES

NOTES

NOTES

NOTES

NOTES